1725

745.2

QUEENS GATE SCHOOL
133 QUEENS GATE
LONDON SW7 5LE
TEL 071-589 3587
WITHDRAWN

DESIGN**TOPICS**

Human Factors

Steve Garner

QUEEN'S GATE SCHOOL
133 QUEEN'S GATE
LONDON SW7 5LE
TELEPHONE:
WITHDRAWN

Oxford University Press

INTRODUCTION

Successful designing requires a knowledge of the intended users. Well designed artifacts, systems, and environments are easy to use and understand – both for individuals and for groups. Existing resources in the area of ergonomics are often too advanced for students who are beginning to develop their design capability.

The Human Factors of Design presents an introduction to the physiological, the psychological, and the sociological aspects of design but in a straightforward manner. The book can be used throughout secondary studies of design and technology but is aimed particularly at the 14–16 year age group. It is generously illustrated and provides pupils with a wide range of assignments throughout the text.

Steve Garner 1991

Oxford University Press, Walton Street, Oxford OX2 6DP

Oxford New York Toronto
Delhi Bombay Calcutta Madras Karachi
Petaling Jaya Singapore Hong Kong Tokyo
Nairobi Dar es Salaam Cape Town
Melbourne Auckland

and associated companies in
Berlin Ibadan

Oxford is a trade mark of Oxford University Press

© Steve Garner

First published 1991, reprinted 1992

A CIP catalogue record for this book is available from the British Library.

All rights reserved. This publication may not be reproduced, stored or transmitted, in any forms or by any means, except in accordance with the terms of licences issued by the Copyright Licensing Agency, or except for fair dealing for the purposes of research or private study, or criticism or review, as permitted under the Copyright, Designs and Patents Act, 1988. Only those pages bearing the instructions © *Oxford University Press: this may be reproduced for class use solely for the purchaser's institute* may be photocopied accordingly. Enquiries concerning reproduction outside those terms should be addressed to the Permissions Department, Oxford University Press.

ISBN 0 19 832783 8

Typeset in News Gothic by
Tradespools Ltd, Frome, Somerset
Printed in France by Pollina, 85400 Luçon - n° 15019

Acknowledgements

J Allan Cash pp 10, 30, 39, 42; **S&R Greenhill** p 48; **J Gregory** p 47; **J Hopkins** p 35; **M O'Brien** p 27; **Watches of Switzerland** p 39.

All other photography by **Steve Garner**, **Chris Honeywell** and **Richard Stevens**.

Every effort has been made to contact the author of the raw data from which the anthropometric data on pp 60–61 are derived. If due credit is required it will be included in subsequent printings.

Illustrations by **Tony Ansell**, **Colin Elgie**, **Linda Jeffrey**, **Peter Richardson**, **JonesSewell** and **Julie Tolliday**.

CONTENTS

QUEENS GATE SCHOOL
133 QUEENS GATE
LONDON SW7 5LE
TEL 071-589 3587

People and design

If you have already experienced working in design and technology you will understand something of the design process. You will know that the activity of designing involves the consideration of many things. Understanding the nature of the problem is very important, and so is exploring a number of alternatives. Not only must a solution overcome the problem, but it must do so economically and safely. The materials that are chosen to construct the final design must be suitable ones, and the method of manufacture should be appropriate to both the forms and the materials.

The design process is never easy, as many of these considerations appear to be in conflict with each other. In short, the designer – or as is more usually the case, the team of specialists responsible for designing – have to find a path through a maze of competing factors.

This book is largely concerned with one particular group of factors. These deal with the limitations and abilities of human beings. In our increasingly technological world they are a vital concern for designers.

They are the **human factors** of design.

You may have come across the term 'human factors' in other books and not understood how it could help you in your technology studies. This book is intended as a clear and simple introduction to the human factors requirements of the design process. Understanding the human factors of design will assist you in devising better solutions to design problems. This book will introduce you to many important considerations.

A variety of people engaged in the development of such products as cars, household goods, computer software, train interiors, and shopping precincts have argued that the human factors are the most important group of factors when designing. Even though production, material, cost, aesthetic, and marketing factors are very important to the success of an item or system, designers are increasingly realizing that the human user must lie at the very centre of the design process. If a manufacturer makes a product that is unsafe, uncomfortable, or presents the user with some other problem then that product fails in the most basic sense. This opinion is represented in the diagram below.

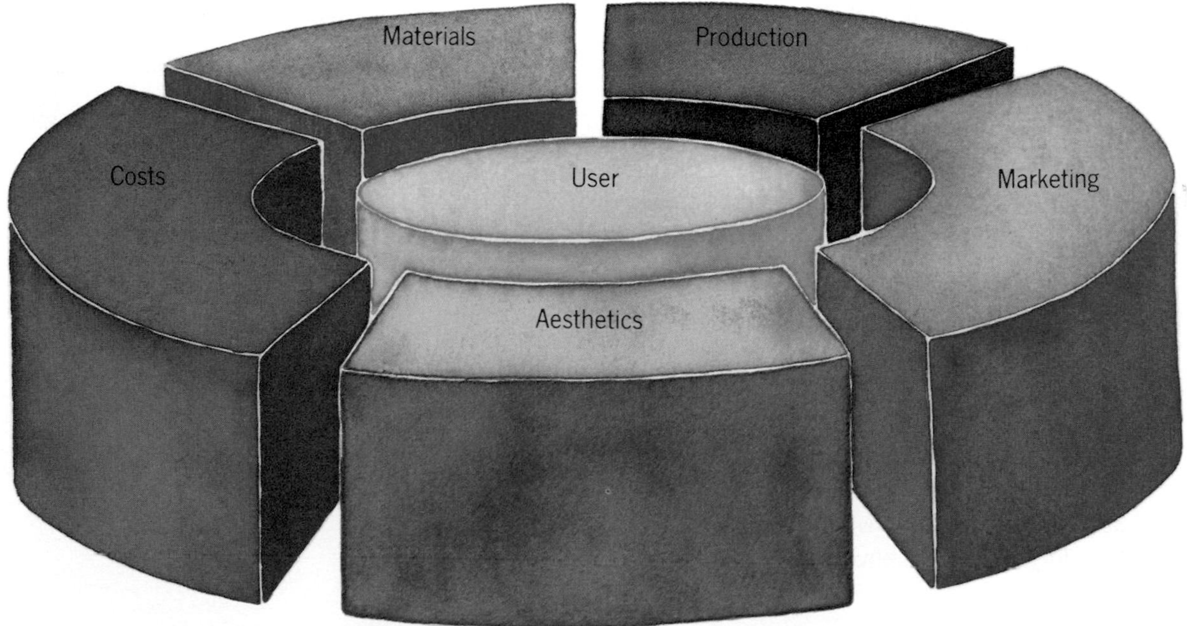

Designing involves many factors, but the user must be the central concern

Ergonomics and human factors

Many books that you will need to use in your design and technology studies will refer to the area of **ergonomics**. The word is relatively new, and was coined to assist the definition of a number of wartime studies that were taking place around 1940. These studies involved the scientific examination of people operating various pieces of military equipment, such as transport and communication systems. They were amongst the very first formal investigations into the human factors of the machinery, equipment, and other products that the human race surrounds itself with.

Ergonomics today

Ergonomics is simply the special title belonging to a family of activities. These involve the scientific analysis of the human aspects of design and designing.

In America the term ergonomics is rarely used. Americans usually refer to this area more directly as human factors engineering. This book will follow their example and refer to human factors, because the term makes a direct reference to the central concern for designers – that is, us as human beings. When reading other books that deal with this area, particularly English ones, bear in mind that the two words can mean the same.

Early ergonomic studies

The word 'ergonomics' is credited to Professor Hywell Murrell, who joined the Greek terms 'ergon', meaning work, and 'nomia', referring to management or organization. With the development of a professional body of researchers, the term ergonomics has gradually come into more general use, particularly in design-related occupations such as architecture, engineering, and product design.

Ergonomics includes a variety of associated activities. They are:

- the consideration of human beings in the creation of products, equipment, and environments;
- the development of procedures for performing work;
- the evaluation of the things people use.

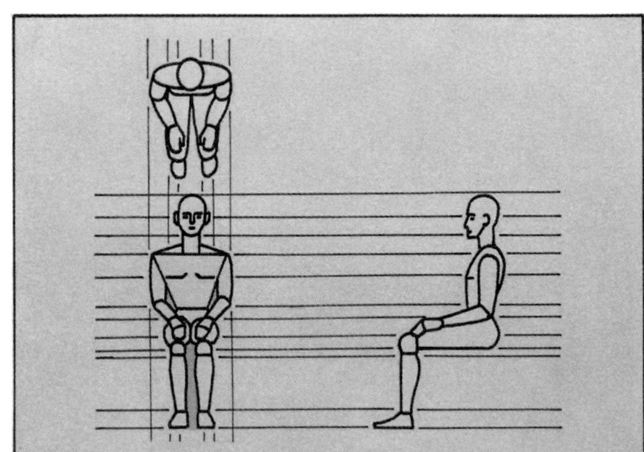

Figures used in ergonomic studies

The earliest human factors

The consideration of human factors in design dates back thousands of years, although formal research techniques are relatively new. Even the earliest human tribes fashioned their tools and hunting implements into shapes that were comfortable to hold or throw.

Their clothing also reveals attention to simple human requirements. It must have taken great skill to prepare and cut animal skins so that they could be wrapped around our curved bodies. Often these basic clothes were decorated with paint or objects to make them even more acceptable to the wearer.

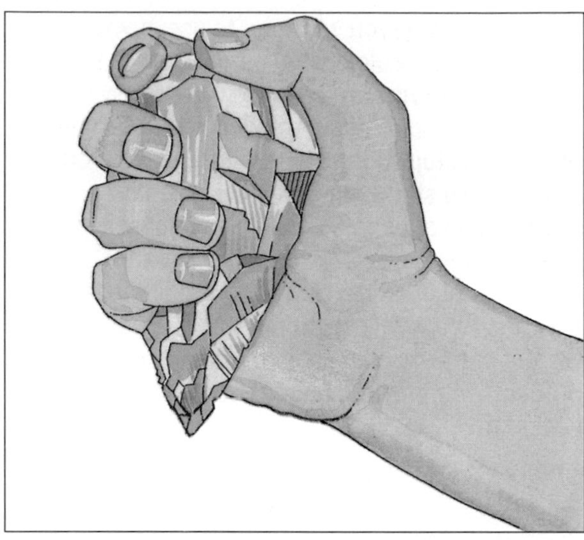

With the development of better metal-forming techniques, the shapes of tools could be improved. Casting and beating enabled craftspeople to produce tools and weapons that were easier and more efficient to use. The Romans considered human factors when they were planning and making products. We can see evidence of this in all manner of items, from the design of coins to the layout of large towns.

ASSIGNMENTS

- Imagine you are a member of an early human tribe. What common items would your people make? How would each item show it was made with the human user in mind? Think about how each one would have been made to suit people's needs and abilities.

- Find out, using a library, what different types of Roman building were like. How do they reveal a consideration of human factors?

Fitting the product to the user

In more recent centuries many people, such as farmers, weavers, and carpenters, have found that the human factors experience of earlier generations has produced good, lasting designs. These people have had to make their own tools and they have shaped them so that they are comfortable to use. Tools that are shaped to fit the user will help to make the job easier and more successful.

The nineteenth-century carpenter's tool shown opposite is a good example of designing with consideration for human factors. This brace and bit has been made to help a skilled woodworker drill a hole through wooden components. It is a convenient size to use and converts easy arm movements into a concentrated cutting action. Even the hand grips are comfortable and smooth.

The shape of the scythe opposite appears very strange. It has a curved metal blade and a smooth, S-shaped wooden handle. The tool only makes sense when you see it being used. The farm worker would be able to cut down hay or grass for many hours each day with slow, graceful sweeps. This design has evolved over hundreds of years. It reveals that our ancestors paid a lot of attention to getting the human factors of design correct in the products that they made.

The person/product interface

The scythe and the brace shown on the previous page are simple products. They work well because they have been designed to suit the size, shape, and ability of the people who will use them. It is vital that designers understand this relationship or **interface** between the product being used and the people who use it. As products become increasingly complex, designers must work in close collaboration with human factors experts. These experts are often referred to as ergonomists, and they have the necessary skills to research and analyse the interface.

Such an interface is found in all designed products that are to be used by people. These can range from very large or complicated products such as a building to very simple items such as a plastic cup.

The human factors of design are closely concerned with examining this person/product interface. It is a term that will often occur in this book so it is important to study it carefully.

Think about the example of the farm worker using a scythe. It involves a person and a product that make up an interface, and their combination has results. The table below shows this.

This example can be the starting point for a table of investigation. It is important to remember that with some products there will be more than one interface. For example, the scythe has an interface both with the farm worker and with the crops being cut. However, this book focuses on the first of these – that is, the person/product interface.

Examples of this interface surround us in our daily lives. For example, brushing your teeth involves you as the person using the toothbrush or product. There are interfaces both between your hand and the handle and between the bristles and your teeth. Each of these has its own result.

Study the table below before you attempt the assignments.

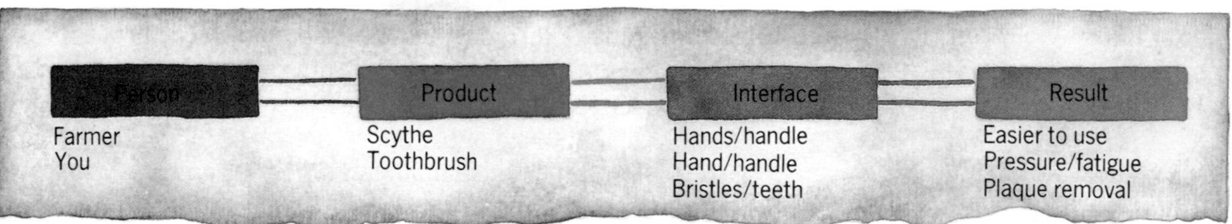

Person	Product	Interface	Result
Farmer	Scythe	Hands/handle	Easier to use
You	Toothbrush	Hand/handle	Pressure/fatigue
		Bristles/teeth	Plaque removal

The person/product interface and its results

ASSIGNMENTS

- On a copy of the table above, list some more examples of the interface between you and the products in differing situations. Do some of your examples involve more than one person/product interface? What results do the interfaces have?

- Imagine you are in each of the following situations, and use your copy of the table to help you describe the different person/product interfaces that you might come across. There is more than one interface in each situation:
  a) using a public telephone. **b)** mending a bicycle puncture. **c)** visiting the dentist.

- Visit shops and a museum to find an example of an everyday modern product and an old version of the same thing. You could study a modern washing machine and an old twin-tub, for example, or an electric drill and a hand drill. What human factors have been considered in each of their designs? Compare these factors.

Three types of human factor

Although some examples of the person/product interface are quite simple, such as brushing your teeth, there are others that are far more complicated. For instance, driving a car requires being comfortable in the seat while reaching the pedals and the steering wheel. It also requires understanding of the controls and the ability to carry out a variety of operations quickly and safely. The human factors involved in simple products, such as the toothbrush or the farmer's scythe, are usually mostly concerned with the physical sizes and shapes of people – for example, how well people grip or how their arm muscles move or work. These factors are known as **physiological factors.**

Design for psychological factors

Many products and activities involve a great deal more than physiological factors. Someone using a microcomputer or driving a car is involved in activities that are far more complicated than brushing your teeth. These activities have physiological factors, but the people involved also have to interpret information and make judgements. The designer of the computer software or of the car can make this easier if he or she takes into account another group of human factors, based on human understanding. These factors have more to do with the brain than the body, and are termed **psychological factors.**

Design for physiological factors

Some designers, such as architects and town planners, also need to consider the social interaction of large groups of people. The design of a housing estate or a supermarket, for example, requires the design team to consider this area of human factors. These are the **sociological factors.**

All designers have a responsibility to acknowledge the people they are designing for. Designers must cater for physiological differences in those who are to buy and use their products, but if designers are also sensitive to the psychological and sociological factors the design may be much more successful. This book attempts to reveal how a designer can improve the person/product interface by considering all these human factors of design.

The following chapters present these physiological (body), psychological (brain), and sociological (group) factors separately.

Design for sociological factors

The living and working human body

The human body has evolved over many millions of years. During this time it has become well equipped to do certain activities. Hunting and food-gathering were only successful with strong, agile bodies. Practical skills such as building a shelter and weapon-making required accurate hand control.

In our highly technological age, we rarely undertake such basic activities. Our new tasks depend, however, on body styles that have not changed significantly in thousands of years.

Modern tasks like this rely on the way the human body has evolved

Whether we are at home, at work, or just relaxing, it is important that the products we use relate to the actual dimensions of our bodies. It is possible to buy some products such as spectacles, clothes, or tennis racquets in various sizes, and these offer more suitability. However, we share the great majority of our products and environments with people of all shapes and sizes.

Can you think of any situations where products that are offered in a single size can cause difficulty in use?

How does a designer know what size and shape to make all of these products? How does he or she find out about the physiological human factors? There are books available that present part of this information. Some of the more useful measurements appear near the end of this book in the form of charts. However, human factors research requires more than simply looking at books. Designers must get involved in their own experiments and studies of humans as users.

Averages and means

The charts towards the end of this book show measurements gathered from a wide sample of people. From statistics like these, **averages** can be calculated which are useful to designers.

The figure plans in Chapter 6 for example, are not taken from any one particular person. Their sizes are meant to represent the average person who might sleep, relax, or work in that room, and so they combine both male and female measurements. This technique of using an average or **mean** is a great help in planning general space requirements.

We cannot all be average, though, so the technique does have some disadvantages. For example, a car that was only designed for average-sized people would result in tall drivers being excessively cramped and short drivers finding difficulty reaching the controls!

Look around you in the classroom or next time you are out in the street. People are different shapes and sizes. Some are tall and thin, others are short and fat. They are all equally important to the designer, but to produce individually tailored products would be expensive and time-consuming.

Most manufacturers set their machines to make items in great numbers. By doing this they can produce them much more cheaply than if they had to produce many different sizes.

A park bench will be uncomfortable to some people and yet other people will find it just right.

ASSIGNMENTS

- Each of us has a unique body. There are many ways it can differ from the bodies of the people around us. Make a list of ten physiological ways in which human beings normally differ from each other.

- Identify five products that are available in different sizes so as to take into account our common physiological differences. What types of size variation are available? Do manufacturers of fashion clothes cater for everybody? Are there any products that you find inconvenient because of size?

- What difficulties might occur at home or at school if designers only considered the average person? Start by considering the size of doors.

People need space

All designers have to undertake research into the sizes and capabilities of the people who might use their final designs. For example, a designer of furniture will need to find out many human dimensions to design chairs that are comfortable for a wide variety of people. Similarly, architects must consider human measurements, and these often include the sizes and capabilities of children as well as of elderly and disabled users.

During the early stages of an interior design project, the team often use a scale drawing of the plan of the building to help them achieve the best layout for the furniture. On this plan they place paper shapes that represent the furniture to the same scale. This allows the designers to determine how much space would be left for people to walk, sit, or undertake any other activity.

In the field of product design, three-dimensional models or two-dimensional images on a computer screen can help designers assess suitable sizes and shapes for their products. But how do designers know how much space to allow?

Developing a product so that it can be used easily and safely by a wide variety of people is not as easy as it may first appear. The example of the interior designer provides a good introduction to an analysis of this type of problem.

The diagram below shows a plan view of a large office in a commercial building, using standard architectural symbols for the desks, chairs, doors, etc. This drawing has been produced to a scale where 2cm represents 1m, or (written another way) a scale of 1:50. It represents the exact size of an intended office. This allows the precise spaces between furniture to be measured. The designer can estimate the success of this layout if the scale plan view includes human figures also drawn to a scale of 1:50.

Larger scale versions of these figures are shown on the next page. You have the opportunity to construct your own layout and figure plan in the assignments there. Any scale can be used with this technique, but it is important to be consistent in any one layout.

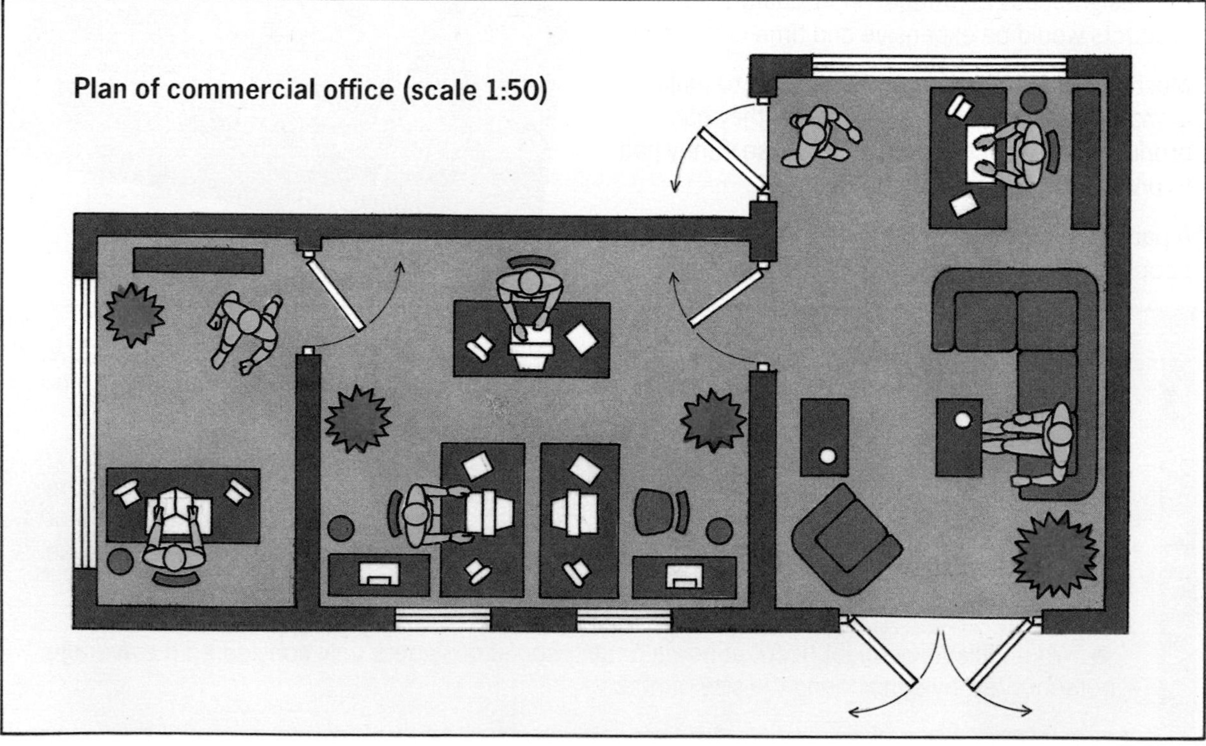
Plan of commercial office (scale 1:50)

ASSIGNMENTS

- This involves you in planning a layout for a room in your own home. Select any one room and make a scale plan drawing of the size and shape of it. Appropriate scales would be 1:10 or 1:20.

Using a library, look up the standard architectural symbols for furniture, doors, windows, etc. Measure the major pieces of furniture in your room, such as chairs, beds, baths, tables, or work-surfaces, and on a separate piece of paper draw plan views of these. Make sure that these are drawn to the same scale as your room plan. Add the appropriate figure plan by tracing one shown below, again to the same scale. Then cut out your drawn shapes.

Your task is to try different arrangements of furniture that are suitable for your room. Use the figure plan while you do this, and do not forget to consider the doors and windows in your proposal. When you are happy with one layout, stick each of the pieces down.

Can you propose a better layout than the existing one, taking into account the users and their activities?

What did you consider important when planning the use of your chosen space? Think back over the different arrangements you made. What did you like or dislike about them? Why did you choose your final layout?

- Choose a public area, such as a shopping centre, library, or bus station that you know. What problems of human use can you identify with the design and layout of this area? Can you suggest improvements? Do your improvements cause any new problems?

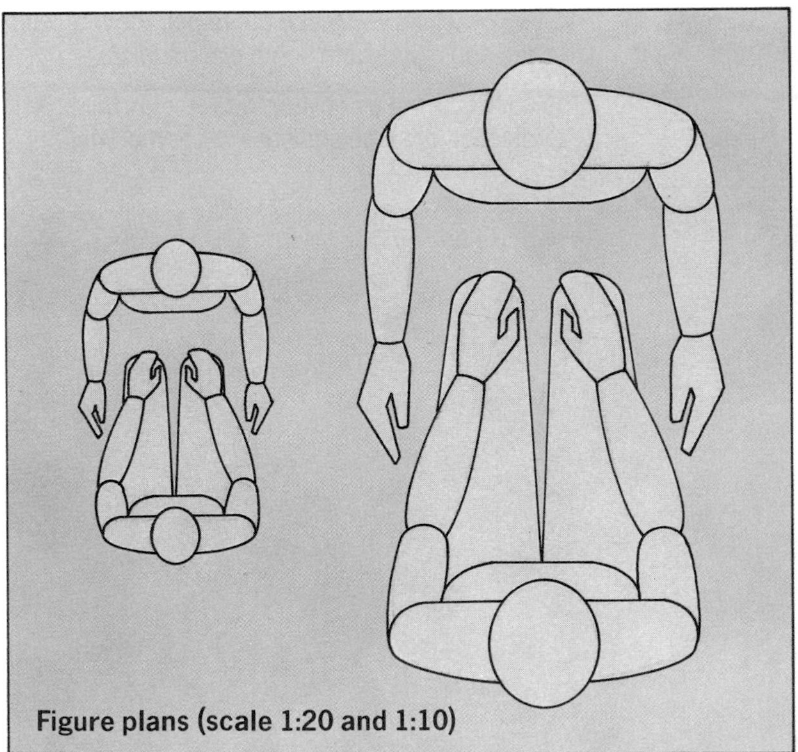

Figure plans (scale 1:20 and 1:10)

Designing for groups

A constant problem for the designer of mass-produced products is the conflict between designing for as wide a variety of people as possible and, at the same time, helping the manufacturer to keep production costs down. If you study the physiological factors of design, you will see how this problem may best be resolved. The development of a multi-media workbench for a school design room is an ideal example for study.

The workbench is to be used by a small group. Students similar in height to the seven shown below could be found in most schools. If you had to design one bench that was comfortable for all of them to work at, how would you decide on its height?

Would you make it for the shortest person, and expect the tallest to bend right down? Would you build it so that the tallest person could use it comfortably, and expect the shortest to reach up higher? Or would you place the bench top between the two and cause both some discomfort?

The answer is not as obvious as you may think. An examination of some statistics will reveal why.

Percentiles

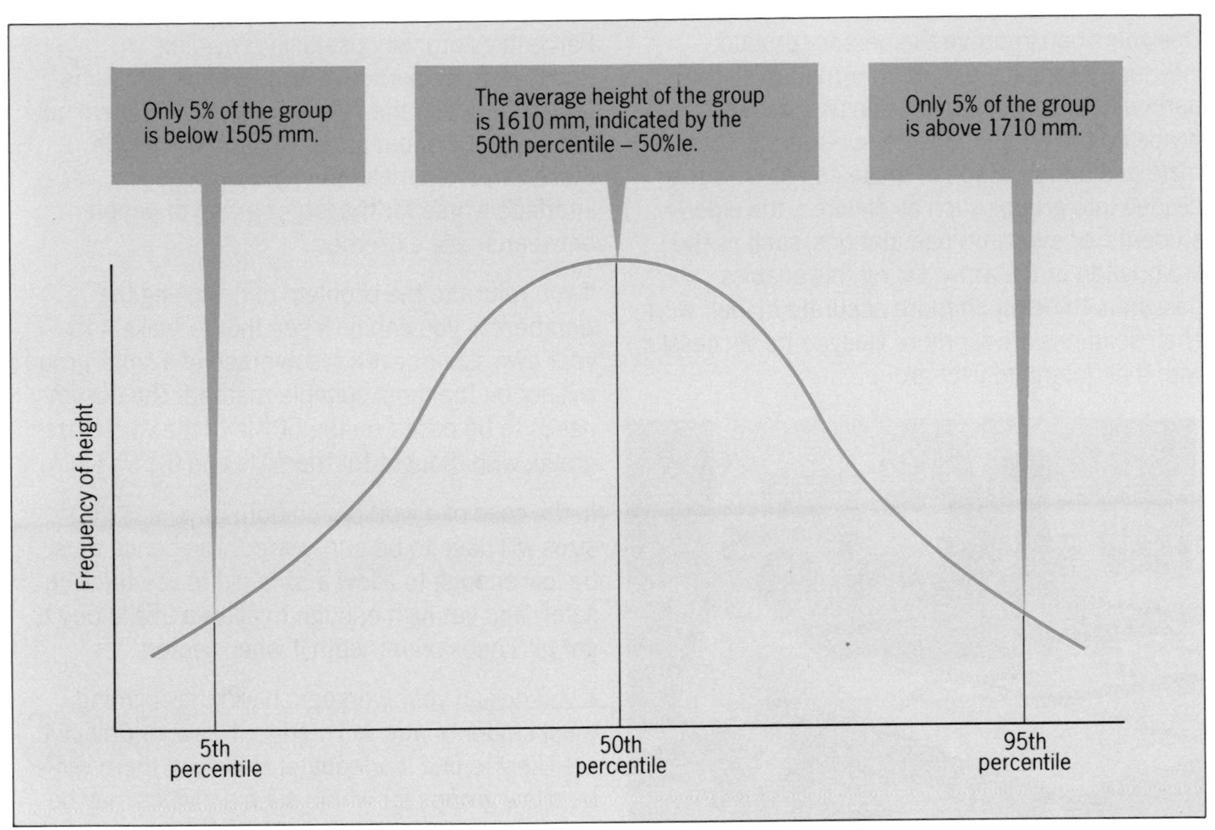

Percentile information as a graph

If you look at the group of seven people opposite you will notice that the increase in height between one person and the next is not the same in each case. The three people in the middle are very nearly the same height. The people beside them are a bit shorter and taller respectively, and it is only the ones on the ends who differ considerably from their neighbours.

If you were to take a very much larger group – let's say 1000 women in the age group 19–65 years – you would notice a similar distribution of heights. That is to say, there would be a great many people around the middle or average in their height, with relatively few who were very tall or very short. If this distribution were represented as a graph it would look something like the one above. Note that height is indicated on the horizontal axis and the frequency of women at these heights is indicated on the vertical axis.

This graph shows that there are relatively few women in our society who are below 1505 mm tall – only 5 per cent of our group. Designers refer to this point as the 'fifth **percentile**' or, written another way, 5%le. Similarly, there are not many women over 1710 mm tall – 95 per cent of our group are less than that. Hence this is referred to as the 'ninety-fifth percentile' (95%le).

By far the majority of our group will be nearer the average women's height of 1610 mm tall. This point, mid-way between the 5%le and the 95%le, is known as the 'fiftieth percentile' (50%le) or the 'mean'.

It is important to remember that no one is 'average' in every respect. A person who is equal in height with the 50%le may have the width of the 95%le person and the arm reach of the 5%le person!

Using percentiles

Designers can improve the person/product interface if they have more information on the particular user group. They can use statistics to divide up the population into sub-groups, such as male and female. Each of these can also be sub-divided into groups such as children, the elderly, students, or even into occupations, such as the fire brigade or the army. Doing this enables designers to be much more accurate in their work. Their solutions are far more likely to be successful with their intended user group.

Percentiles are very useful in providing information on particular user groups. Products that lie between the 5%le and the 95%le leave out relatively few of our society. To try to include these can often make the person/product interface worse for the larger group of people between these extremes.

If you return to the problem of designing the workbench, you can now see that to make it to your own size or even the average of a small group will not be the most suitable method. The design needs to be based on the 50%le of the whole user group, with thought for the 5%le and the 95%le.

In the case of a workbench both boys' and girls' sizes will have to be considered. The bench must be low enough to allow a 5%le girl to use the vice safely and yet high enough to allow a 95%le boy to get his knees underneath it when seated.

If you design your workbench with this in mind, most students who will mark out, saw, or drill at it are likely to find it adequate. However, there will be a few groups for whom such activities may be difficult or even dangerous. Making products adjustable is one way for a designer to assist minority groups too.

ASSIGNMENTS

- Very occasionally a designer will not need to consult percentile information. Can you think of a range of examples where a design is undertaken to fit one person only? Why are these products designed like this?

- Produce a frequency chart of pupils' heights. Measure the heights of fifty pupils in the age range 14–16 years. Place these in groups of 25-mm height intervals. Convert this frequency chart into a frequency curve, similar to the one shown on page 15. Plot height on the horizontal axis and frequency on the vertical axis. From your information, work out your 5%le and 95%le. How does your class differ from the percentile heights that are given in the 14–16 age group table on page 60?

  Measure other basic body dimensions, and compare them in the same way.

- Designers require more information than simple body dimensions. Think, for example, about the factors involved in using a computer or driving a car. Try to list as many as you can. Starting from these activities, what other human capabilities would it be useful to measure and convert into percentile tables? On what projects might such information be used?

Further use of scale figures

The room planning exercise on page 13 involves the use of a human shape drawn in plan. Designers often use another view of the human body to help them develop and evaluate design ideas. This is a side view. It is made carefully to a suitable scale and presents the information from a chosen percentile. Its scale largely depends on what design task is being undertaken. It may vary between 1:20 scale (about 85 mm high) and a full-scale figure (about 1700 mm high). Such a figure is often called an **ergonome.**

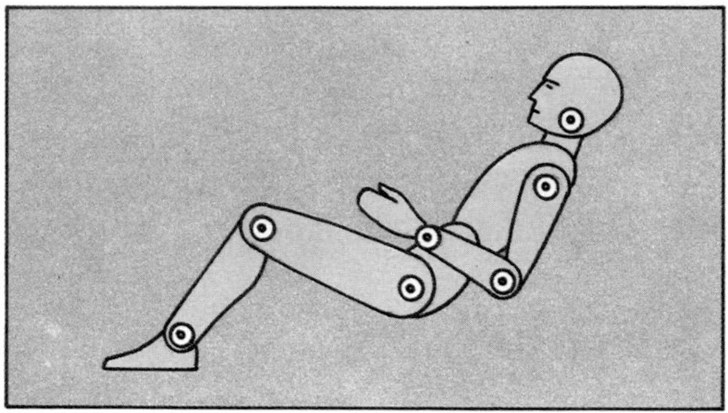

An ergonome

The photographs show design teams using different scale figures alongside their design ideas. The vehicle designers opposite are using two full-size ergonomes to check that the car interior will be suitable for different drivers. One represents a 5%le female and the other a 95%le male. The figures can swivel in approximately the same places that a real human body does – that is, at the neck, shoulder, hip, elbow, wrist, knee, and ankle. By using figures such as these as well as their drawings, the designers can get an early idea as to whether drivers will be able to reach the pedals and the controls, not touch the car roof, and sit comfortably in the seat, as well as many other features. If the design looks promising a full-size model of the product can be made and tests undertaken with a variety of volunteers.

The engineers opposite are also using a movable figure. This one is on a much smaller scale than the one the car designers are using. It is being used as a rough guide to ensure that a machine operator will be able to see all of the instruments and dials as well as reach all of the controls. Because the figure is movable it can be made to bend down low and reach up high. The human factors in any firm proposal from this team would be more rigorously evaluated than this, but the figure is a useful guide at the early stages of a project.

The assignments on the next page will provide you with your own movable scale figures. They will be useful in a number of future design projects.

Making ergonomes

ASSIGNMENTS

● Printed on pages 62–3 are all the components necessary for you to make up movable figures or ergonomes 1:10 the scale of a real person. Two outlines are provided, one showing the 95%le male in the 19–65 age group and the other showing the 5%le female in the same age group.

Follow the instructions below carefully. If you have access to a photocopier you can avoid steps 1, 2, and 3.

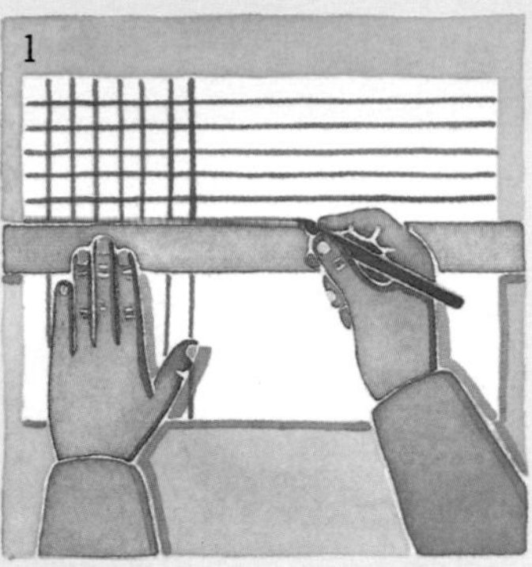

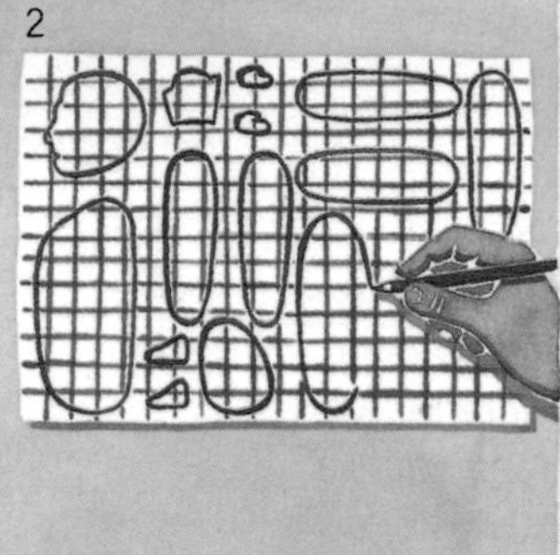

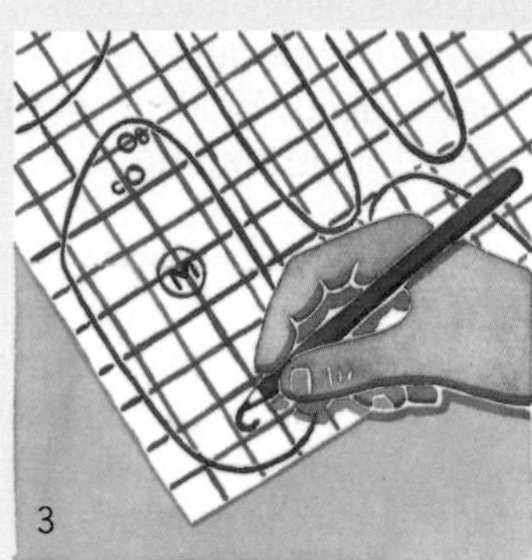

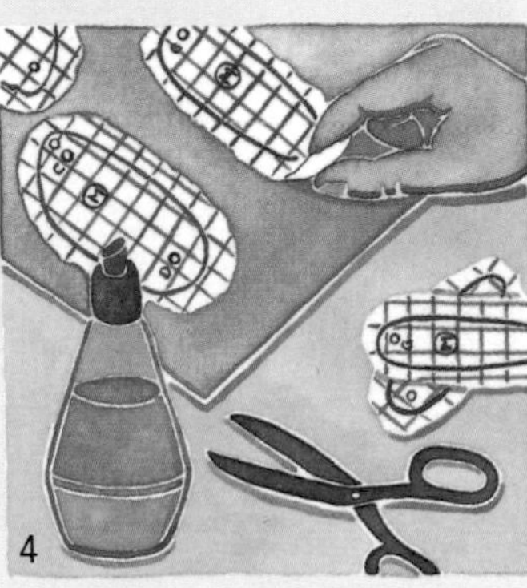

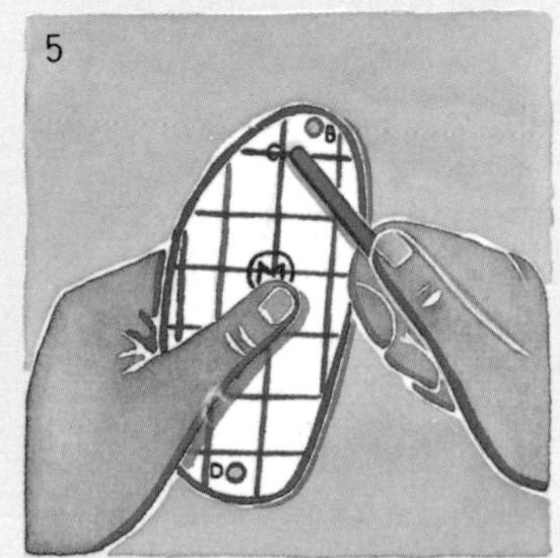

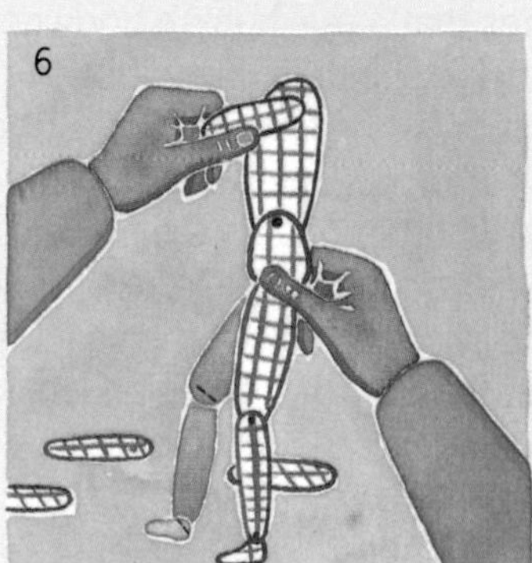

1 Divide up a plain sheet of A3 paper into a 10-mm grid (picture 1).

2 For each figure, copy each of the body parts onto this sheet. Use the grid lines to help you reproduce each one to exactly the right size (picture 2).

3 Mark in the positions for the holes. Copy the appropriate reference letter next to each hole (picture 3).
If you are making both ergonomes take care not to mix up the body parts.

4 Cut out these paper shapes and stick them down securely onto thin card, such as a breakfast cereal packet (picture 4).

5 Now carefully cut the shapes out of the card and make a small hole in each of the places indicated (picture 5).

6 Finally you will be able to assemble your figure with the use of thirteen paper fasteners. Place letter A on the head over letter A on the neck and secure this with one of the fasteners. Repeat this with letters B–I until you have assembled every joint (picture 6).

You now have your own scale figures. Because you have copied these figures from the book, yours are also 1:10 scale, but it is possible to make them bigger or smaller. If you had drawn a 5 mm grid and then copied the body parts yours would have been half the size of the ones in the book – that is, 1:20 scale. If, on the other hand, you had drawn the grid 20 mm in size, your figures would have been twice as big – that is, 1:5 scale.

When you have completed your own 1:10 scale figure you may wish to attempt the assignments below, which will provide you with a full-size ergonome. Design offices often have their own full-size ergonomes to work with. These ones are usually cut out of thin plywood or rigid plastic sheet to make them more durable.

When using these ergonomes it is important to remember that they come from statistical averages. Think of fat, thin, tall, and short people when you are designing.

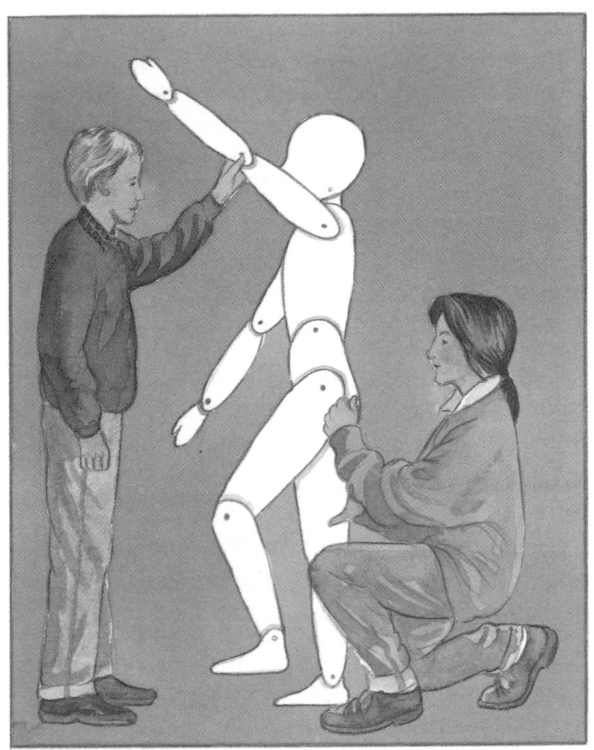

ASSIGNMENTS

- You will need a lot of strong plain paper for this exercise. You could use old rolls of wallpaper left over from decorating a room. The objective is to make a full-size figure like the ones used by the car designers shown on page 17. Because it is very big this would make a suitable project for group work.

Select your group's body parts from one of the diagrams on pages 62–3. On the large sheets of paper draw a grid, with each square measuring 100 mm by 100 mm. How much of this grid you need will depend on which part of the body you are to make. Copy out the part as explained for the 1:10 scale version and check it carefully before you cut it out. These paper parts can then be stuck onto card (discarded cartons are a good source) and cut out, or assembled as they are.

- Using the above technique, construct an ergonome based on either:
  - **a)** the 50%le of your class, or
  - **b)** any percentile taken from the 14–16 age group information given on page 60.

- Look again at the photograph of car designers on page 17. What else is it possible to examine using a full-size ergonome? Look around your school and a local public area, such as a shopping precinct, for products you could investigate with your ergonome. Work out how you could best use it for a detailed study of one of these products.

Then carry out the study, and record your findings. How useful did you find the ergonome?

Anthropometrics

So far this chapter has attempted to make you think of the need to investigate the user-group for any particular design project. The sections on percentiles and scale figures presented you with people's dimensions, but where do we get these measurements from, and can we trust them? This section on **anthropometrics** takes a closer look at the information that is available for designers to use, and presents ideas for collecting your own anthropometric data.

Like the term 'ergonomics', the word 'anthropometrics' is relatively new. It is made up from Greek terms that refer to human beings and measurement. Anthropometrics is the special term used to describe the scientific collection of measurements taken from a wide variety of men and women. It is a very important branch of human factors research.

You have already seen on page 5 how some of the earliest formal studies of the human factors of design were made on military equipment. Similarly, the first anthropometric studies were based on soldiers, sailors, and aircraft pilots. It was relatively easy to collect such information as height, weight, and arm reach for these people, but the findings are only of limited use to us as designers.

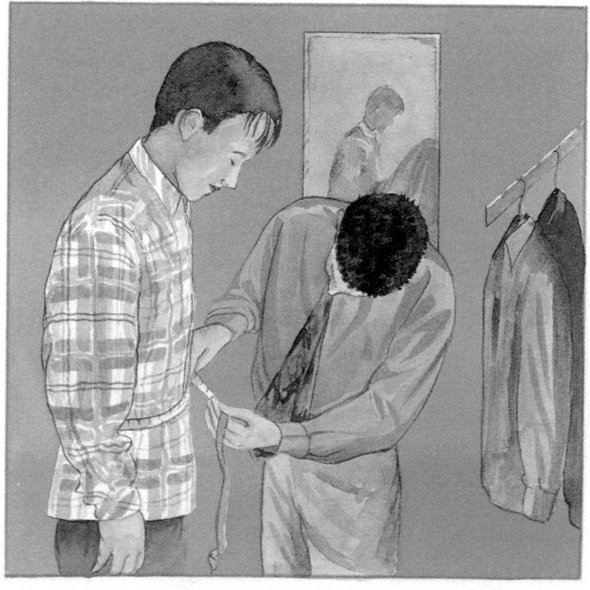

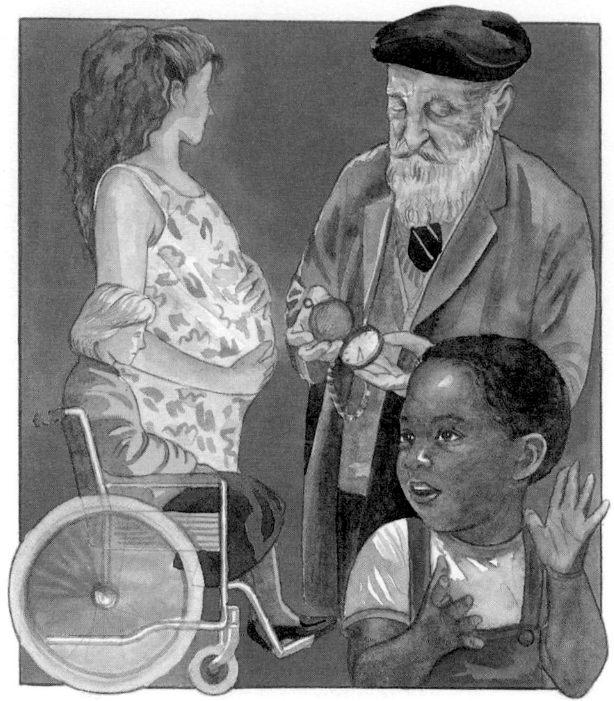

Even though many thousands of people may have been involved in these early studies, it is important to remember that military personnel are not representative of all members of society. They include no old people, no children, no pregnant women, and few people with any significant disability. The information was drawn only from fit, young people, and this severely limits its application in design for society in general.

There have been more recent studies that set out to overcome this, but a great deal of anthropometric data that is available in human factors books must be treated with caution. If in doubt, check the source of the measurements when using books of anthropometric data.

Anthropometric measurements surround us daily. We use them to buy the correct shoes, gloves, and shirts; we can specify a grip size for a tennis racquet; even bicycle frames can be bought according to leg length. In all of these cases it is important for the measuring to be accurate and consistent. The collection of anthropometric data is always carefully undertaken so that its application is meaningful.

Collecting anthropometric data

Ergonomists have probably paid more attention to the measurement of the human body than to any other area of human research. They have identified a large number of points on the body where measurements can be reliably and repeatably taken. You may have been measured in a shop when you last bought some clothes, but the scientists need to record a great deal more information than this. The diagrams on this page indicate how detailed their anthropometric information can be.

The letters in the illustrations identify basic body measurements. They correspond with the letters used in the anthropometric charts towards the end of this book. Use the charts as a key.

A number of anthropometric studies have set out to record body dimensions exactly, so their subjects have worn few clothes. Designers therefore often have to make allowances for clothing. Shoes or boots will make people taller, overcoats will make them wider, and protective clothing can greatly increase the users' 'actual' size. For example, workers who wear safety helmets will require more headroom in buildings and vehicles.

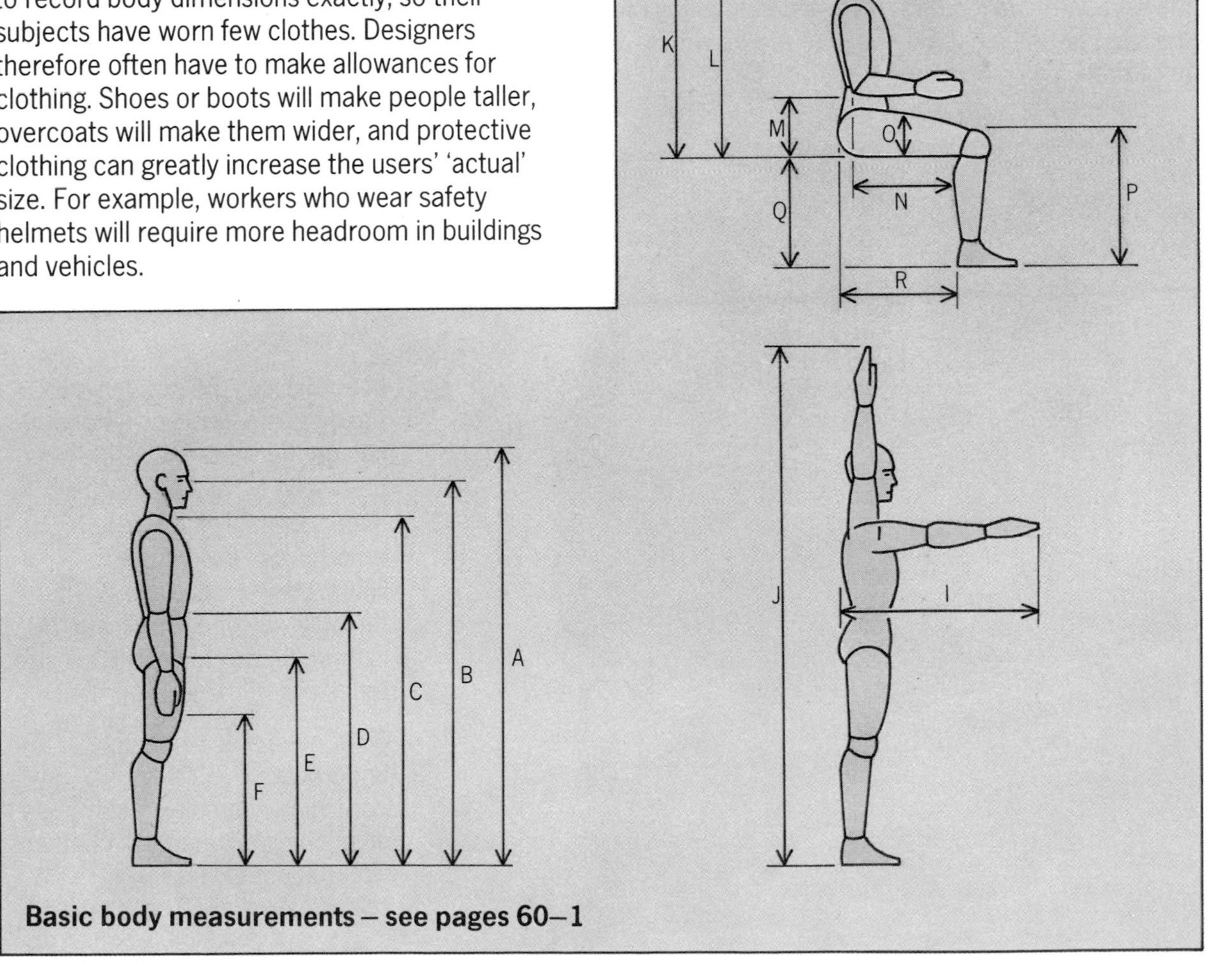

Basic body measurements – see pages 60–1

Dynamic and static anthropometrics

Anthropometric surveys provide designers with a great deal of useful information. However, in real-life situations people rarely stand still or sit in formal, **static** positions. The human body is jointed and our muscles allow us to make complex movements. Throughout the day we are usually moving – leaning forward, turning our heads, bending our knees, or making any of thousands of other movements. When using products we adjust our grip, stretch upwards, or reach around. Our lives are a series of **dynamic** activities.

Designers may use both static and dynamic information to improve particular person/product interfaces. For example, designers of computer workstations must consider a wide range of human factors, but especially the heights of both the seat and the computer, the reach forward to the keyboard and the disk drive, and the turning of the head or body that may be required for writing or talking.

Kitchen planners will need to allow for people bending down or reaching up to storage cupboards, turning from the cooker or sink, and standing to prepare food.

In both cases the designers will need to establish how far people can comfortably extend themselves. That is, designers need to establish the **reach envelope** of the people for whom they are designing. Often the only way of determining this is through user trials with full-size mock-ups of the environment.

A car mechanic working underneath a vehicle has a particularly complex reach envelope. Can you think of other occupations that display complicated reach envelopes?

Other human measurements

Ergonomists do not only study the basic body dimensions, such as height. Tables of percentiles are available on the sizes of such parts as feet, head, and hands. They reveal, for example, comfortable grip sizes for different groups, which may be applied in the design of products like handtools or bottles. These studies also provide the basic information for developing products such as childproof containers.

Physiological studies also include examinations of people's strength – the force they can exert when doing different tasks. These may range from pressing a lever with the foot to changing a lightbulb. Experiments such as these have to take into account people moving their body, or changing their grip to get a stronger action. They are complicated by the 'dynamic' nature of the activity and are the subject of specialist research into **biomechanics.**

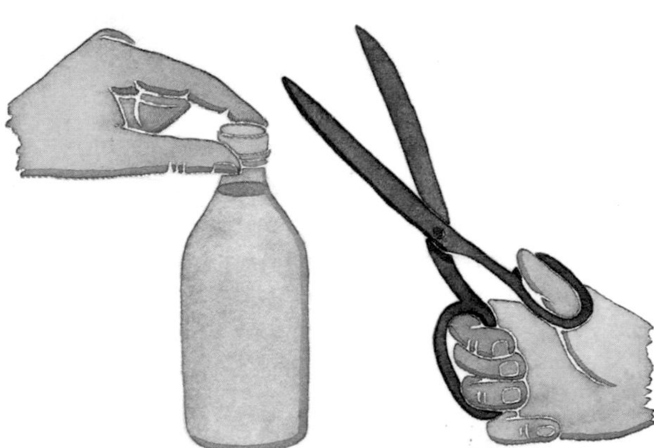

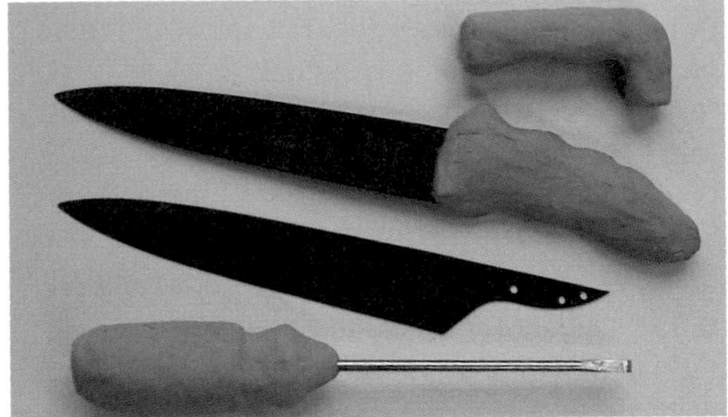

Handles tested as full-size models

Just as the designer of the workstation or the kitchen may choose to use a full-size mock-up, so investigations into biomechanics will often use full-size models and prototypes. The handles of the walking stick, knife, and screwdriver in the photograph have all been modelled and tried out with the relevant user-group. This enables the design team to learn more about the users' limitations or abilities.

Our hands are perhaps one of the most important links in the person/product interface. Designers often require information on hands, such as their size, strength, and manoeuvrability. Handles on doors need to be easy to grip and turn; suitcase handles should be comfortable for small or elderly hands; and operators have to use machines with a variety of knobs, buttons, and other hand controls.

So important is this last area that it will be examined in closer detail on the next two pages.

ASSIGNMENTS

- Look around you at school, at home, and in your local area. Try to identify products where static anthropometric information appears to have been most important to the designer, and those where dynamic anthropometric information has been of greater importance. Make two lists of these designs, one for static information and one for dynamic.

- Select three of the body dimensions from the 14–16 chart near the back of the book. Plan, undertake, and record your own static anthropometric survey of your class or school for these dimensions.

How do your measurements compare with those in the chart? What reasons can you think of to account for any differences?

You need hands!

Our hands are required daily to control tools and products. Hi-fi systems, handtools, cookers, television sets, and motor vehicles all present us with a means of controlling their various operations by hand. The designer of these items has two objectives which are closely related. They are:

- to make the form, layout, and function as easy to understand as possible.
- to design forms and arrange components that suit the physical limitations of the intended user-group.

The first of these objectives is largely concerned with how our brains receive and interpret information. Therefore this aspect of control is examined separately in the next chapter, on psychological human factors.

The second objective lies clearly within the area of this chapter, that is, the anthropometric or physiological human factors. The designer must consider a number of these physical factors when designing products requiring control.

On this page you can see a variety of people operating controls. Some, such as the lock gates, require the user to push with his or her whole body. Others, such as the shaver, can be operated with a flick of the thumb.

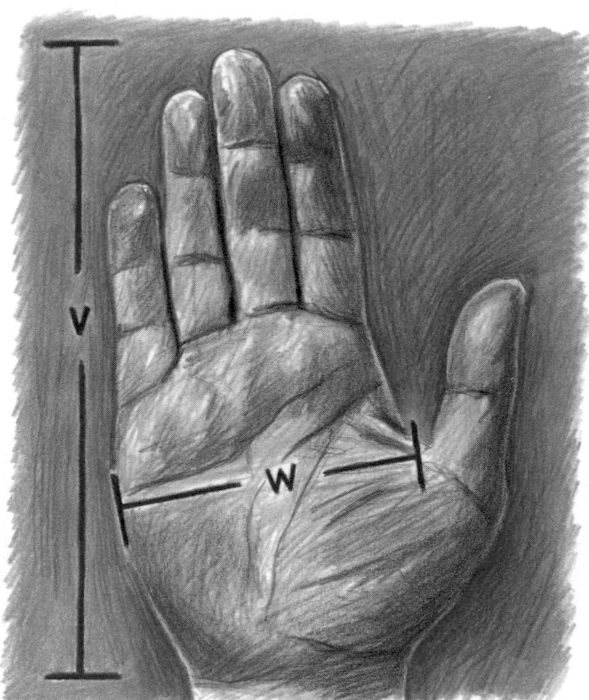

V = hand length, W = hand breadth

It may seem obvious that controls should relate to the user's body dimensions, but many products fail even this simple requirement. You may have noticed miniature calculators in which the buttons are so closely packed that even the smallest hands have difficulty operating without error. Similarly, some industrial workers have great difficulty using their machines when wearing protective gloves or boots. In both of these cases the designer must closely examine the intended environment and the real limitations of the user.

The choice of controls, such as rotary or switch, will largely depend on the nature of the task. People tire easily if they are expected to exert great force. The designer can reduce this effort by skilful design. Many books are available on the mechanical advantage available through controls, but there is no substitute for making a full-size mock-up and testing this with the intended user-group.

The size, shape, and texture of controls play an important part in successful design. They can easily be too big or too small, especially if they are to be used for fine tuning. For turning applications requiring some strength, both texture and shape help in achieving a better grip. Bottle tops and screwdriver handles show this. Supermarket trollies and sailboards now use wider diameter handles to assist pushing and turning.

ASSIGNMENTS

- Choose any one hour between getting up in the morning and going to bed at night. Think about your activities and produce a list of every product that your hands come into contact with during this hour. Are any of the products especially hard or easy to use? What makes them so?

- Each product may have its own unique controls, but many are broadly similar in function. Groups of controls such as levers, knobs, and switches can be identified. Select one of these groups and collect between twelve and twenty pictures of different controls. Investigate the job each one does and how well it does it. Would a control from another group do the job more or less effectively?

Prepare a short analysis of these controls based on your own observations.

The human mind and understanding

The previous chapter presented the need for designers to consider the shapes, sizes, and physical abilities of a wide range of people. However, to achieve improvements in the person/product interface the designer has to consider more than just the user's body. The successful products are those that are easy to understand.

It is important to remember that 'products' can include instruction manuals, exhibitions, and computer software. The physical aspects of such products are only a small part of the design. Design teams have to be aware of how the human mind works when confronted by machines, products, environments, or systems. They have to be aware of the **psychological factors** of design.

Sensing information

In every activity we undertake our brains are receiving information. Watching television and making a telephone call are obvious examples, but people also receive information when they sit in a chair or open a tin of beans! Pressure on the legs and back provides information when seated. People are aware when they have opened a tin correctly because of information sensed by hands, eyes, ears, and nose. Our senses continually provide information, and clever designing can harness this potential.

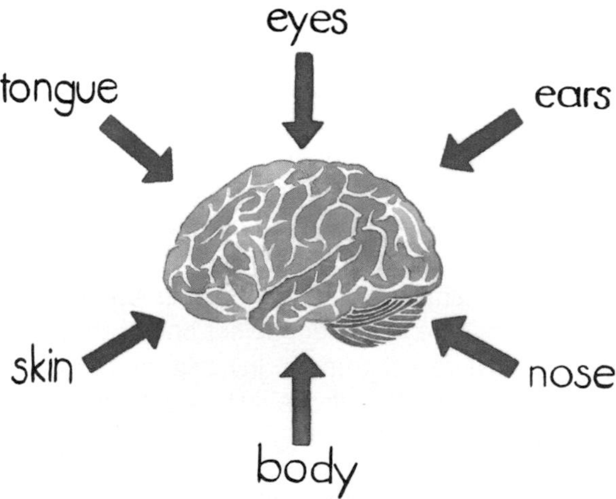

The brain and its channels of information

Our bodies have evolved to provide a variety of types of information, each via specialist sense organs. These are:

- eyes – visual information such as movement, shape, and colour;
- ears – auditory information such as noise, sounds, and speech;
- nose – olfactory information on smells;
- tongue – tastes of sweet, sour, salt, and bitter;
- skin – tactile information such as touch, pressure, and temperature.

In addition to these senses it is worth noting a general ability of the human body to feel movement, such as that experienced on a fairground ride. This is called the kinaesthetic sense.

The illustration opposite shows a human figure whose sensory organs are redrawn to a size that represents their importance. That is, those senses that provide the greatest amount of essential information are drawn biggest, except for the eyes – they are the most sensitive sensory organs and should really be drawn the size of oranges! However, each sense depends upon the brain to collect and interpret signals so that we may adjust our actions accordingly. This interpretation process is a very important consideration for the design teams who develop many of today's products.

Take the common activity of driving a motor car. Millions of people worldwide find it relatively easy, and yet in reality it is very complicated. A driver must watch the road ahead and turn the steering wheel accordingly. Mirrors relay information from behind. The driver must listen for other road users, and the vibration of the car provides further information through the body and hands. To understand speed a glance at a dial or other display is required, and at any time a light may flash to warn of low petrol or oil, or of a high temperature in the engine. In addition to all of this, the driver may be talking or listening to the radio!

You can see that in addition to the physical comfort of the seat and the easy reach of the controls, the driver needs to be able to interpret information that is received through the senses. The designer can make this easier by studying the psychological factors of design.

Designing for the senses

All products and systems need to be understood before we can use them successfully. Some, such as a garden spade, are obvious, as their shape indicates where the hands and feet should be placed. Others, such as cookers and hi-fi equipment, have multiple functions, and therefore it is very important for them to be designed to communicate information clearly.

As with the spade, the shape of any product can help us to understand how to use it. The steam iron in the photograph has a form that communicates where it is to be held. Similarly the camera is shaped to dictate the way it is used. In recent years this phenomenon of the meaning of shape has received close scrutiny by designers. They refer to it as **product semantics**.

Many products require us to interpret more information than just shape. The steam iron, for example, provides information about its temperature and its mode of operation – steam on or off, temperature suitable for wool, etc. If users interpret this information wrongly they may burn themselves or damage the clothing. In order for users to interpret information correctly, designers employ a variety of devices to provide information and instruction about their product. Some of these take the form of words or symbols and may be found in instructions or graphics. Others rely on colour, careful display design, and even texture to communicate intention.

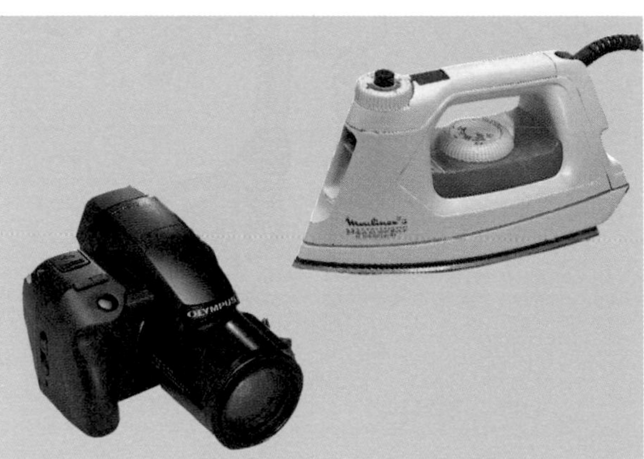

ASSIGNMENTS

- Remember the details of a short walk or bicycle ride that you have had. What senses did you use and what information was received?

- The importance of our sense of smell is undervalued. Visit local car showrooms and ask if you may sit in a selection of new cars. Working in pairs or groups, write down your description of the smell of each new car. How do your comments compare with those of another student?

  What other products have a distinctive smell?

- Select one machine from a school workshop or science room. A lathe, cooker, or power supply would be appropriate. What information is communicated to the user about the machine's functions? How is this done? How effective is the communication?

- Choose three very different shops in your community and discuss the image of each. What are the factors that influence its visual image? (Again, you should think about what information is communicated, and how this is done.)

Displaying information

Transferring information from machines to people is not easy. Human beings are fallible and the information may be missed, forgotten, ignored, or misinterpreted. Therefore designers need to understand something of human **perception**. They need to get involved with the psychological field of understanding information.

We are all familiar with traffic lights that provide us with essential information, but coloured lights are used in many other situations. A red light may show that a radio or computer is switched on, and flashing lights immediately draw people's attention. Some machines even use flashing buttons to indicate clearly where to press. Where simple communication from a product to a user is required, such as 'on' or 'off', simple indicator lights may be the best solution. More complicated products may use more complicated indicators – for example, hover lawnmowers often provide a spinning indicator on the top of the machine to warn users of the hidden moving blade.

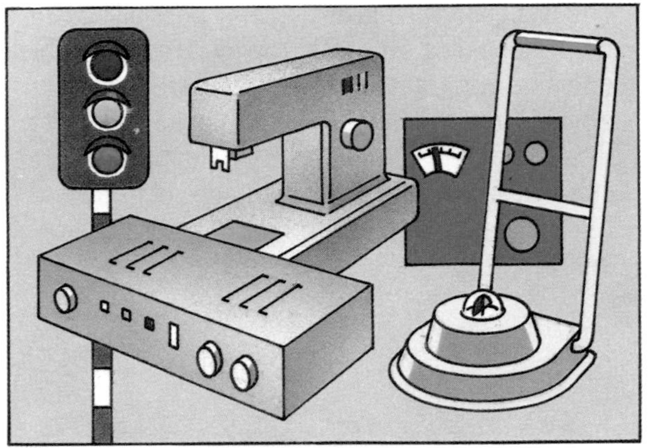

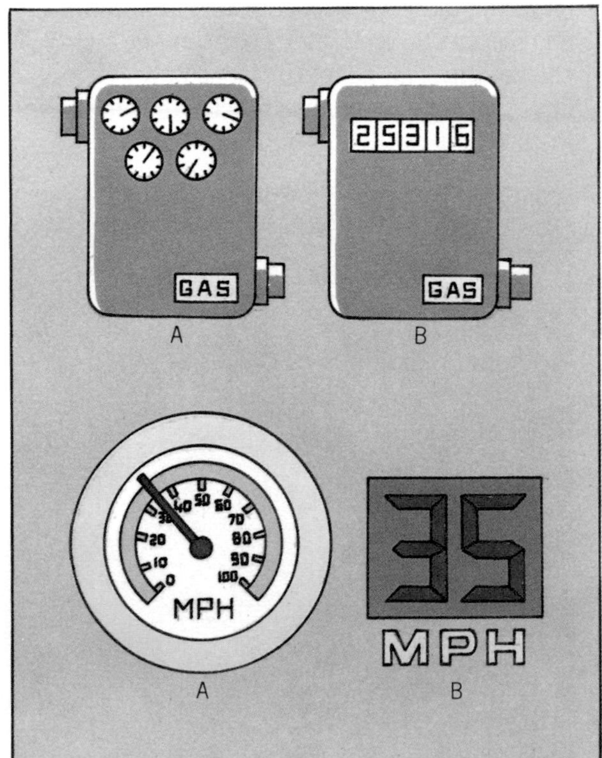

Analogue (A) and digital (B) displays

Analogue v. digital

Where information is more complex, involving quantities or rate of change, then a single indicator light is not enough to communicate it. Two common designs for domestic gas meters are shown opposite. The dials on each of them provide the same information on how many units of gas have been used. Which of the two versions do you find easier to read, and why?

A similar problem arises for the manufacturers of advanced sports cars. Opposite are two designs for a speedometer. Both of them have advantages and disadvantages, and the designer must be aware of these.

It is likely that where numbers can change so fast that they cannot be read easily, as in the speedometer, the dial or analogue version (A) is preferable. With analogue dials the viewer is left to judge the actual reading from the position of a pointer or needle. However, where slow changes occur or where precise measurements are required, such as in the gas meter, people may rather have the clarity and precision of the digital display with its bold numbers (B). Both analogue and digital displays should be clear, simple, and uncluttered.

Many modern cars do use digital speedometers. How have the designers overcome the difficulty of numbers changing so fast?

Control layouts

The designer must investigate all possibilities before deciding on which display is most suitable, and it is important to remember there is no obvious answer. Sometimes analogue and digital displays are used together – for example, in power stations – providing the advantages of both. Alternative designs for such displays are shown below.

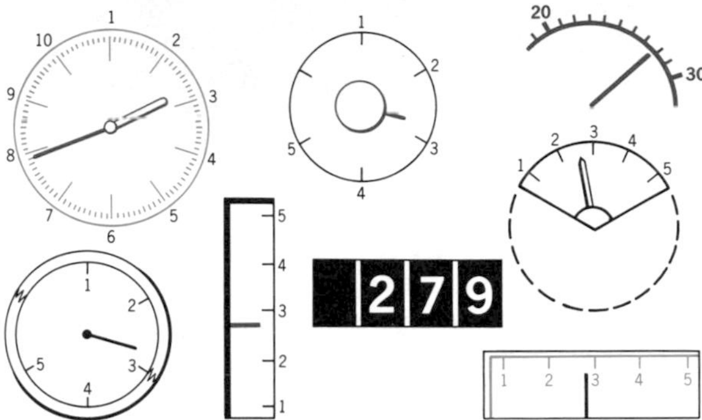

Different designs to display the same information

With the widespread availability of computer technology, the suitable presentation of information is a design issue for us all. Visual display units (VDUs) are not limited to digital figures, and much research still needs to be done on our psychological requirements for the presentation of information on these screens.

Where many displays or controls are grouped together, the designer must pay particular attention to distinguishing one piece of information from another. Varying the type of display or the use of colour often helps people to read information accurately. Experiments have shown the advantages of placing the most important or frequently used displays close to the centre of the operator's vision. Similarly, controls with similar functions should be placed close to each other, to assist comparison and avoid mistakes.

We read books in European alphabets from the top left corner to the bottom right corner. Perhaps it is logical that control procedures should also follow this left-to-right progression.

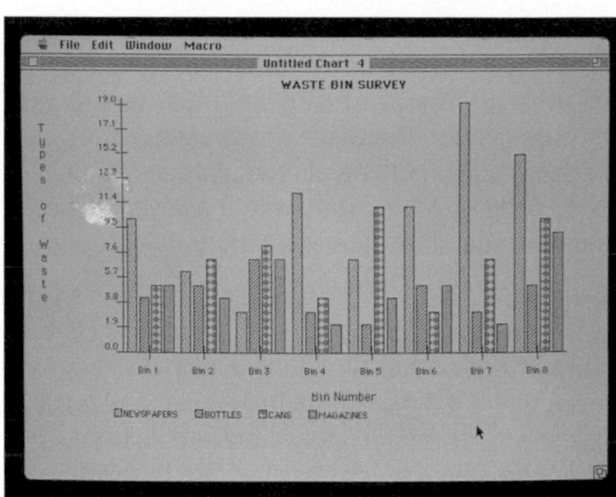

In very complicated systems, such as the cockpit of an aircraft, audible signals may be used to back up visual information. Buzzers or even computer-generated voices provide information through a less crowded sense organ – in this case the ear. Good control design allows the operator to respond to information easily and quickly. However, there will be a human **reaction time**, and this can be important. For example, a motor car can travel for quite a distance between a driver seeing a hazard and reacting by pressing the brake.

Using other senses

The previous chapter presented the need for considering people's physical limitations when using controls. However, the design of the controls themselves can do much to affect the successful use of any control panel. The size, shape, and texture of controls can provide information that supplements what is seen. For example, pilots of military aircraft need to make fast in-flight decisions. The use of shaped and textured controls allows the pilot's sense of touch to play a part in the rapid selection of levers and controls.

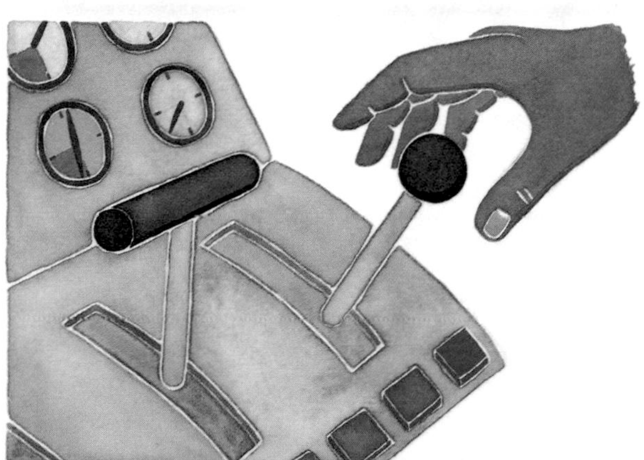

In more routine situations, switches and buttons can provide **feedback** to the user by offering some resistance or making a noise. Designers of many domestic products are beginning to apply the ergonomists' psychological findings. Control panels are now providing a variety of information in a readily understandable manner that does not depend solely on sight.

ASSIGNMENTS

- Make a list of every sense that you use within any 5-minute period and note the cause of each stimulus. (For example, the stimulus for your using the sense of hearing might be a sound such as someone speaking or a bell ringing.) Then, working in pairs, take it in turn to be blindfolded and describe the textures in your local environment. This may be done inside or outside. Your partner should note your descriptions down.

What evidence can you find of texture being deliberately used in products?

- Construct a full-size drawing of the controls on the panel of any domestic product. A washing machine, television, or hi-fi amplifier would be appropriate. Cut out these shapes and rearrange them according to the guidance on these two pages. Can you improve the arrangement? Why is your proposal better than the original? Remember to design for the needs of everyone in the user-group.

- Find a simple domestic electrical product such as an iron, a kettle, or a radio, and describe how information is communicated from the product to the user. **Do not plug it in.** Use drawings and notes to describe your findings.

Symbols

Instructions, warnings, and controls all exploit symbols. They can be found in many products including leaflets, photo booths, chemical containers, and car dashboards. They are particularly important for international products, as they can communicate simple messages without requiring the user to speak a foreign language. They are also useful in situations where people may not be able to read.

Symbols are quicker to read than words, but it is important that everybody interprets any given symbol the same way. Misunderstanding the meaning of a symbol could have serious results. It may be annoying to press the wrong symbol on a television remote control, but it would be disastrous if a crane operator mixed up the symbols on the levers and buttons in the cab.

To reduce these mistakes, very thorough studies have been undertaken. Detailed user trials have provided general opinions on the meaning and clarity of images, and these have been used to design standard symbols for use by manufacturers. A selection from the British Standards Institution (BSI), which sets up and maintains standards on construction, technical terms, and symbols, is shown here.

No smoking

Eye protection must be worn

Smoking and naked flames prohibited

Head protection must be worn

Pedestrians prohibited

Hearing protection must be worn

Do not extinguish with water

Foot protection must be worn

Not drinking water

Hand protection must be worn

Some BSI symbols

Symbols must communicate their message easily and without confusion. It is important to achieve a strong contrast between the symbol or 'figure' and the surface or 'ground' onto which it is put. Often this is achieved by using a silhouette of the intended subject. It should not look similar to any other symbol, otherwise the user may interpret the control wrongly.

Symbols should only be used for the simplest of instructions. Where complexity is unavoidable, the designer must consider using a combination of instructions, training, product semantics, and symbols to improve the person/product interface. Ideally the product should be as foolproof as possible.

Many manufacturers continue to apply symbols or graphics to products for reasons other than instruction or information. Images or lines are often used to balance or visually link areas of form together. Graphics can work simultaneously with factors such as shape, colour, and texture to create a particular **product identity**. This may have, for example, a sporting or hi-tech look. A few examples of the effects of graphics are shown on this page.

ASSIGNMENTS

- Imagine your school is to play host to a large group of overseas students. Design a symbol for each of the following areas that can be used on signs throughout the school:
  - **a)** the staffroom.
  - **b)** the technology areas.
  - **c)** the caretaker's room.

Consider the problems such a group might have and design one other symbol for an area of your choice.

- Examine any modern product which uses graphics, from a crisp packet to a computer. Identify where graphics have been used to communicate instructions.

Imagine the product without graphics. What are their other functions on your chosen product?

- Company logotypes or logos – the emblems or trademarks that identify companies – are a form of symbol. They are commonly found on lorries, advertisements, and products. Find a logo that you like and describe it in detail.

Why do you think the designers chose that particular image? Think about the type of company that uses it, and how easy it is to recognize.

Colour

Colour surrounds us in our environment to such an extent that we often take it for granted. However, if you examine your surroundings you will see that many products exploit colour to do a job of work. The police officer on traffic duty can be made more conspicuous if he or she wears a fluorescent green or orange top, while military equipment can be camouflaged by applying the appropriate paint.

Other uses of colour rely on interpretation. The traffic lights that are seen on major roads use only red, amber, and green to provide instructions, and many machines follow the accepted interpretation of green for 'on' or 'go' and red to indicate 'stop' or 'danger'. Similarly, electrical wiring uses colour to distinguish between live, neutral, and earth.

How does the colour scheme change the room?

Colour and human perception

Colour can influence mood or feeling. The choice of colour for wallpaper, carpets, or furnishings can result in a house feeling warm and welcoming; cool and spacious; or oppressive. Although the dimensions of a room do not change, our brains interpret the colour to provoke a judgement or feeling. Interior designers and architects deliberately choose a colour scheme that provokes the feelings they wish us to experience. In general, red, orange, or brown colours will appear warmer than the cooler colours of blue or green.

Colour in product design is becoming increasingly important, especially in the creation of product identity. The photographs show three illustrations of this. The personal stereo has an outdoor, fun image largely as a result of its yellow casing. The electric toothbrush possesses a clean and hygienic medical image, primarily due to its simple white colouring, and the lawnmower associates itself with healthy lawns because it is bright green. In each of these cases colour is having a major effect on the way we see or perceive the product. Designers of fashion clothes, high street shops, and advertising literature all exploit such associations with colour.

HEATELECTRIC

Designers can deliberately use colour to make a product easier or safer to use. Switches, controls, and handles can be made more obvious if they contrast with their surroundings. Similarly, colour can draw attention to instructions or warnings. The use of lighter colours can even fool people into thinking a product weighs less than it actually does, whereas dark colours tend to have the oppposite effect. Colour can link areas together, and this is useful in complex designs such as large machinery.

Further evidence of the psychological importance of colour is the widespread occurrence in Britain of dressing babies according to sex – blue for boys and pink for girls!

Great care must be exercised in the use of colour, however, as colours can have different connotations in different countries or for different ethnic groups. For example, white may be perceived as a fresh, healthy choice for a European product, but it denotes mourning in some Middle and Far Eastern countries and to some religious groups.

Hue, value, and chroma

Successful use of colour depends upon the designer selecting not only the correct **hue** – red, green, blue, etc. – but the appropriate darkness/lightness of colour, or **value**, and strength of colour, or **chroma**. To neglect this can often reverse the expected effect.

Colour is only one influence in our perception of products. Form, texture, materials, graphics, association, etc. all exert a simultaneous influence, and a designer must wait until all are combined in a prototype before attempting any significant assessment of the total effect.

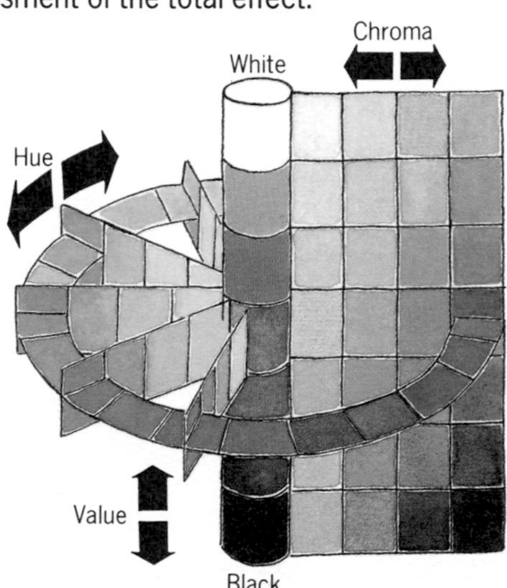

People make judgements because of colour, although few understand it. It affects the purchase of electrical products, cars, and furnishings as well as fashion goods such as clothes. It even influences sales of foodstuffs – most major food manufacturers spend large sums of money on both the packaging and the actual food to achieve the correct psychological effect with the colours of pizzas, yoghurt, cakes, etc.

There is still very little hard evidence on the properties of colour and even less on its effect in product design. Design decisions regarding colour are largely a matter of informed personal judgement, backed up by user trials to test the effect on a variety of people.

ASSIGNMENTS

- Find some examples of colour being used to do a job of work at school, at home, or in your local area. Can you find certain hues that are often used for the same sort of job (such as red for 'stop' or 'danger')? What effect do the value and chroma have in each example?
- Cut out a variety of colour advertisements from magazines. How is colour used in the products? How does it affect the image of the advertisement?
- Select any three products you wish. These may range from clothes, such as ski jackets, to technical equipment. Produce a number of identical drawings of each and use colour to alter the image of each one. Think about why you chose certain colours and evaluate your proposals.
- Prepare a simple meal using harmless food colouring to change the image of each item. For example, you could have blue baked beans and red mashed potato! Try out your meal with blindfolded volunteers. Then show them the colours. How do they react? Which colours are most liked and disliked?

Interpreting the environment

So far in this chapter the emphasis has been on the psychological human factors involved in the design and use of domestic products. However, our brains interpret information in many other situations. When we are out in the street, inside a building, or doing a job of work our brains are interpreting information that is received through all the senses (see page 26). This information from the environment can have a dramatic effect on our work and leisure.

The potential of colour in a room has already been presented. It was shown to have an effect on the way we saw, felt, or perceived the room. Other types of feeling may come from the temperature, the nature of the lighting, or the type and level of sound. The following sections examine these environmental factors in more detail.

Temperature

Our bodies can usually regulate our temperature in response to the temperature of the environment. When this mechanism fails to work it can have serious consequences. In winter old people risk hypothermia – an abnormally low body temperature that can be fatal – if their bodies cannot make enough heat to overcome the cold around them, especially in underheated rooms. Polar explorers risk frost-bite, involving the freezing of fingers or toes.

Clearly, achieving a comfortable temperature will depend on what clothing people are wearing, and the designer can usually have little control over this. However, the need for protective clothing can dramatically increase a worker's body temperature, and the designer should allow for this. Any design solution to problems of temperature must take into account a variety of requirements, such as the need for special clothing. Similarly, good ventilation may be difficult if heat conservation is a priority – opening a window in winter lets in fresh air but lets out valuable heat!

Interpreting the environment: lighting

Both relaxation and work are affected by lighting. Good illumination is an important requirement for most jobs, and this may be a mixture of general environmental lighting and localized spot lighting. Lighting may also influence mood in much the same way that colour does. An interior can be transformed from a bland or gloomy space into a warm and welcoming environment. Designers for television and the theatre are particularly skilled in creating these illusions with lighting.

Research studies have documented appropriate levels of illumination for a wide variety of activities and situations. There are numerical tables of the findings available to assist designers.

The human eye can adapt to different levels of light. It is possible to see shapes quite well at night provided your eyes have had a short time to adjust to the very low level of light. This adaptation is important; it allows us to walk from a bright street into a dark building, for example.

However, the designer should attempt to avoid the need for the user's eyes to adapt constantly during any activity, as it is likely to lead to eye strain and headaches. As a general rule the level of the illumination should increase as the task becomes more precise. So, for example, a watchmender will require a very bright light onto the working surface, whereas a corridor requires only enough lighting to illuminate the obstacles.

The main criteria for good lighting design are that it should:

- adequately illuminate working areas;
- avoid strong contrasts within the working area;
- avoid glare from bulbs or from shiny materials;
- achieve a balance of lighting that makes the environment pleasant to work in.

Colour rendition

There are many types of artificial lighting. Neon lights provide a distinctive type of illumination that is often used for shop signs, while sodium street lights bathe the whole street in an orange or yellow glow.

Not all 'white lights' are as they seem. The colours of lights from a car headlamp, a fluorescent tube, or a household bulb will each be slightly different. This in turn will affect the colour of the objects being illuminated. Design offices often use special 'daylight' bulbs for studio lighting, so that models and drawings receive the exact colour that is intended.

The brief overview of lighting issues on these pages does not account for every situation. For example, elderly people may require greater illumination on signs and stairways to make up for failing eyesight. Can you think of other examples?

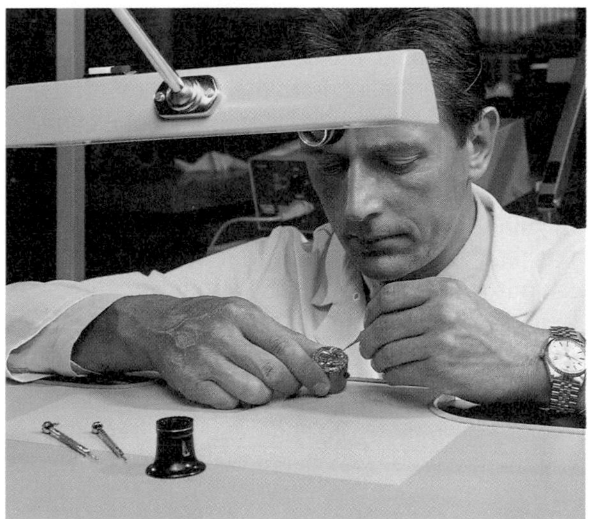

Interpreting the environment: sound

Unlike the eyes, which have a natural cover in the form of the eyelid, the ears are continually receiving information from the environment. The greater part of this sound is ignored, but it can provide vital information about our surroundings. If you have ever listened to music through headphones you will understand the strange feeling of not being able to hear people or other sounds in the room. You may also have experienced the desire to put your fingers in your ears when sound becomes an unwanted noise!

Sound and feedback

We rely on sound to back up other information. For example, if you stroke a cat and it purrs you can be fairly confident in continuing to stroke it. Similarly, you can see yourself activate a switch on an electric plug, but the click adds a comforting confirmation. Turning a key in a lock provides audible as well as visual information. When they do not hear an expected noise, many people's reaction is to examine the silent device for faults!

This confirmation or feedback is an important part of products and systems. Designers need to understand that although many people expect to receive this feedback – especially audible feedback – the great majority will underestimate its importance. It is the designer's task to ensure that relevant 'subconscious' feedback is incorporated into their solutions. The assignments for this section will raise your sensitivity to these psychological factors of design.

Noise in the environment can be extremely disruptive to work and leisure. Low-flying aircraft or road menders with pneumatic drills can cause severe irritation, but any noise that makes it difficult to concentrate or hold a conversation can have a similar effect. Open plan offices often use screens to reduce noise, and factory machinery is usually enclosed with sound-deadening material.

Sound in the environment can also be positive. Many public buildings and exhibitions play quiet, relaxing music, while bird song can add an extra dimension to parks and open areas.

Controls exploit sound and can communicate different levels of urgency. For example, a constant loud bell may indicate an emergency such as a fire, while a quiet buzz can gently appeal for our attention. The noise of a telephone can vary from harsh and annoying to calm and barely audible. Designers must match the sounds of a product to its function and level of importance.

ASSIGNMENTS

- Find a street that is lit at night by orange or yellow sodium lights. Compare the colour of cars there by day and by night. Is your perception of some colours affected more than that of others? List the colours you see by daylight and by the street lights.

- Find five examples at home of sound providing feedback to indicate that an action has been carried out correctly. You will find that this usually occurs where other senses are limited in what they can detect. What types of sound are used?

  How else do products provide feedback?

- The ringing sound of a telephone instructs the hearer to pick it up. In what other products does sound provide instruction? For each of these products, try to work out why sound is used rather than, for example, a visual instruction like a flashing light.

The human group

So far the examination has focused on products that relate to people in physiological and psychological terms. But what of very large design projects, such as a building or even a new town centre? For these the designers need to be aware of a third group of factors. These are the **sociological factors** of design.

People tend to live and work in large groups. Our houses are clustered together, sometimes to form towns or cities, and we travel in groups on trains and buses. Even our leisure time can be spent in crowds at the cinema, a sports event, or a concert. It is important that designers study this, as groups can require very different considerations to individuals.

You may have experienced a crowded situation in which you felt uncomfortable or under stress. It is possible to design our environment so that these feelings are kept to the minimum, to make work more efficient and leisure more enjoyable. The social interaction of people should therefore be a major concern for designers.

The photograph shows a relatively new housing estate. The design team that helped develop this were not only interested in the houses but devised the layout for the open spaces, the roads, and the footpaths. The design project involved the whole local environment.

However, a new path can be seen running across the open land. This path may be a short cut to the shops or link two important roads. You can see that many people prefer this route to the one intended by the designers because they have worn away the grass in this area. It appears that the design team did not anticipate this when they planned the layout of the footpaths.

It may be that new shops or a school have been built since the estate was planned. Major roadworks may have closed or restricted an important footpath. But perhaps the new path reveals that the design team neglected a proper consideration of the sociological factors of design.

Architects are commonly faced with problems associated with large numbers of people. For a large office building, architects not only have to consider physiological factors such as the height of doors or lift buttons and psychological factors such as colour scheme and lighting levels. They also have to consider the sociological factors associated with large numbers of people moving about and working in a series of interconnected rooms. The building and its function may be seen as a **system**, with the people as one component in this system.

Large developments need team planning

The sociological factors within such a system may include:

- different numbers of people at different times of the day;
- maximum densities of people in different areas;
- increased wear in certain areas of the building;
- high noise levels as a result of large numbers of people;
- effectiveness of public address systems, sirens, and bells;
- safety in areas such as stairs and upper floors;
- facilities such as toilets and cloakrooms;
- consideration of handicapped people;
- areas of delays and bottlenecks that reduce the efficiency of the building;
- provision of dining or snack facilities;
- cleaning and maintenance services.

This list provides a very simple overview of the types of consideration that an architectural team might bear in mind when planning the use of their building by large groups of people.

Transport systems

The list on the previous page may also be used in other situations. One example is the design of public transport. The illustration below shows a design for the interior of a standard double-decker bus. The designers had a number of decisions to make concerning the physiological and the psychological factors, but the analysis here is limited to the sociological factors.

If most people were asked to get on and off an empty bus they would probably find it easy. However, imagine yourself doing the same task on a cold, rainy evening with a crowded bus and two large bags of shopping! The task is further complicated if you imagine yourself as an elderly or handicapped person or as responsible for a young child.

The design team had to consider a variety of people getting onto a crowded bus, paying their money and taking a ticket, and then moving to a seat – perhaps while the bus is accelerating forward. Often the other passengers can hinder this movement. Shopping bags or luggage can be tripped over, people may be standing in the way at your stop, or you may have difficulty in attracting the attention of the driver to get the bus to stop.

The designers must consider the bus in use, not empty or as a good-looking drawing. They must consider the social interaction of people and the way that this affects their proposals.

ASSIGNMENTS

- Look around your school or any local area used by large numbers of people. What evidence can you find to indicate that people have changed their environment away from what the designers and planners intended?

- Pick one area of your school that is sometimes crowded, such as a refreshments area or the library. Plan and undertake a study to find out what difficulties people have there at busy times. How could these be overcome?

- Try to visit and observe a large public space, such as a football stadium or a cinema, when it is in use. What sociological factors need to be considered in spaces like this? Use the list on page 43 to give you some starting points for your study.

The design team responsible for the bus in the illustration have made its use as easy as possible for as wide a range of people as possible:

- the entry step is low enough for elderly people to be able to step up;
- luggage space is conveniently located for pushchairs and bags;
- the instructions on the ticket machine clearly indicate what to do;
- central doors speed up the entry and exit of passengers;
- there are plenty of grab rails at a convenient height on stairs and around the seats – safety is vital;
- floors are non-slip.

The vast numbers of people that use public transport involve the designers in another consideration – how to keep the bus clean and operational. This in turn affects the choice of materials such as panelling and seat fabric.

Once the design of a bus is agreed, there is further sociological analysis to be undertaken. Planners must examine the routes for these buses and run them to suit the public demand. If planners do not acknowledge a new housing estate or do not study the different volumes of traffic throughout the day, people will find alternative means of travel. Just as the footpath in the photograph on page 43 was created by the needs of a number of individuals, so people may react to poor public transport by using their own cars, which will create traffic congestion and increase pollution.

Personal space

Human beings seem to enjoy group activities. It has already been noted that we group together at school, at work, and in our leisure activities. The way these groups function, though, will depend on relationships between the individuals.

Look at the illustration opposite. Do you think these people know each other? How can you tell? Compare this group with the people in the illustrations below.

Specialists in this field have studied the human interaction of groups. They have identified a **personal space** that surrounds each of us. It would appear that we allow close friends into our personal space, whereas strangers are kept at a distance.

Such findings are important to designers. For example, in planning the layout of a large office it is important to allow everybody the privacy of their personal space. Screens, plants, and furniture can be used to define the boundaries, while reducing the number of people will decrease pressure on such space. Travelling on public transport often results in the unintentional invasion of personal space, which tends to make people stressed and uncomfortable.

ASSIGNMENTS

- Describe a situation where you felt your personal space was being invaded by people you did not know. How did it make you feel?
- Devise a study to find out how close people can sit in a school classroom and still work in a comfortable and relaxed manner. Try out different arrangements of furniture on other classes who do not know your intention.

Designing for specialist groups

The first chapter presented an outline of the history of human factors research. It showed that the earliest studies were limited to military personnel such as sailors and airmen. Because these groups were not representative of society as a whole, the findings only had a limited application to manufacturing industry. Further studies had to be undertaken involving children, teenagers, and the elderly, from differing social and ethnic backgrounds. More recently, such specialist research has been extended with studies into the requirements of people with a particular disability.

It is probably easy for you to hold your pen or pencil, but if you were an old person with a stiff or painful hand you might have great difficulty in getting your fingers around such a small object. If you are involved in a design project you should think of all the possible people who may use your final solution. Most people would not find it difficult to pick up a bottle of lemonade from a table, but how many times have you seen people, especially children, struggling to unscrew the bottle top? This example highlights the designer's need to understand people's hand strengths and the shapes and textures that could make it easier for all those in the user-group to grip the bottle top.

We are all disabled

The term 'disability' can have a very wide range of applications. It is possible to consider that we are all disabled in some way at some time, if you look at the limitations of the human body and mind. Sometimes the disability is permanent but mild, such as short sight; sometimes it is serious but temporary, such as a broken arm. For some people a serious disability is there for life.

Designing for disability

People with permanent handicaps do not live in another world from those without them. They also have to wash, cook, and go to the toilet, and may want to develop interests at work or leisure. Designers can assist all disabled people in two basic ways:

- They can consider the problems of disabled users when designing products for the mass market, and so help them lead as normal and as integrated a life as possible. (Traditionally people with handicaps have been neglected, because they often fall below the 5%le or lie above the 95%le in studies);
- They can increase the capability of severely disabled people by assisting in the development of specialist equipment and products.

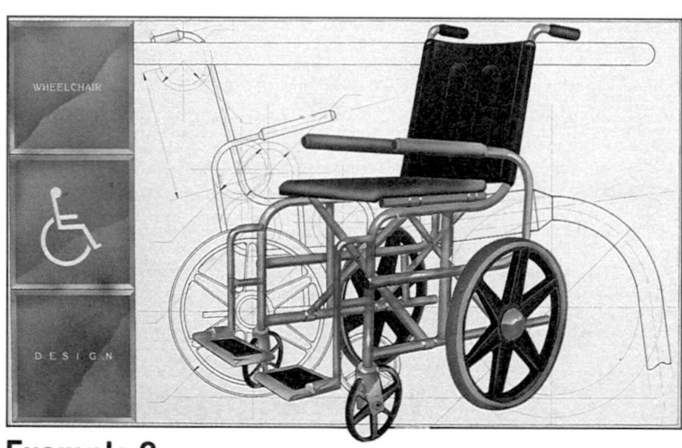

Example 2

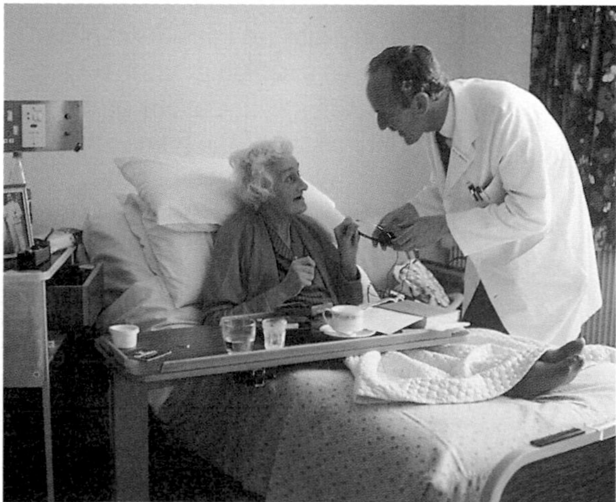

Example 3

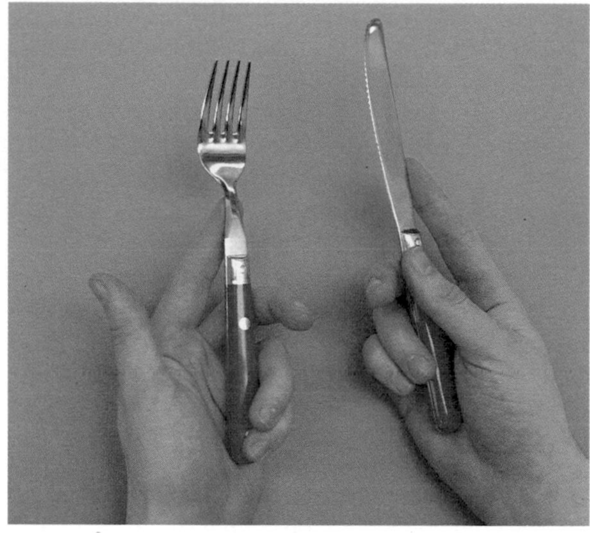

Example 1

The knives and forks shown as Example 1 have a bright, modern appearance and have sold well to able-bodied families. They were first designed to provide a thick, chunky grip for elderly people who found it difficult to hold small items in their hands. The cutlery can be used by both old and young without drawing attention to disability or involving extra cost.

Example 2 shows a specialist wheelchair for a young person with severe physical and mental disabilities. The chair had to provide a number of features and yet have a modern and exciting image. This wheelchair was never intended for mass production. The nature of 'design for disability' often dictates that solutions are produced individually, and this frequently puts off industrial collaboration because of increased costs.

Example 3 shows a specialist table for use in a hospital. An ordinary table would not fit over the bed, so this design slides in from the side. A tilting surface allows the patient to eat, play games, read, or operate a computer keyboard while lying down. The table can be easily cleaned, lowered, and stored, and is adaptable enough to be used by patients with a variety of injuries.

'Designing for disability' involves able-bodied people in discarding many of their preconceptions. It is important to talk with the disabled people you are designing for, and with those who work with them, if you are to discover the true nature of their problems. Solutions should be developed in conjunction with the 'specialists' – the people who find that they cannot turn on a tap, open a bottle, or use a public toilet.

All designers should naturally design for disability. Public buildings can have ramps for wheelchair access as well as steps; signs can be both attractive and legible to the elderly; and toys may be used in a hospital as well as at home or in a school.

There is still little information on the effects of some disabilities. When designing for people with these, you should consider undertaking user trials with full-size models and prototypes to determine the requirements.

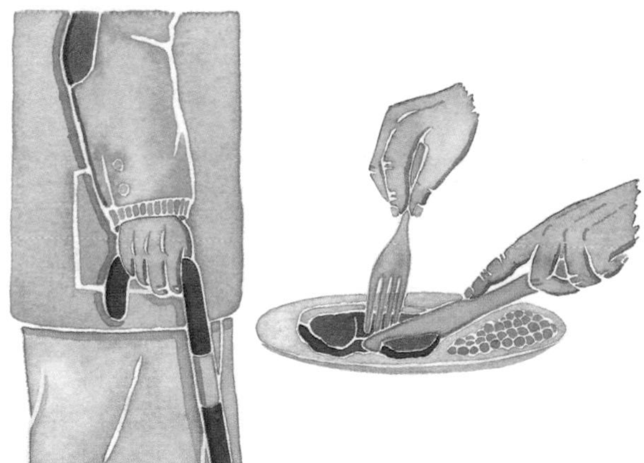

ASSIGNMENTS

- Imagine that a bad accident meant that both your arms were in plaster for a number of weeks. How would this affect your daily activities? List as many effects on as many activities as you can think of.

- Imagine that someone who is fit and able from the waist up but who must rely on a wheelchair for mobility wants to visit your school. Write down any difficulties that he or she might experience. Could a designer help remove some of these difficulties?

Shopping centre redevelopment

Clearly with a design project as big as this the result is the work of a number of specialists, including architects, planners, engineers, and designers. A town centre is the living heart of an area and as such must provide a wide variety of facilities for many people. There are a great many human factors to take into account in this type of redevelopment.

Shops, banks, cinemas, medical services, and sports facilities attract large numbers of people to the town. Public transport must be given access and private cars given somewhere to park. Ideally this should be near to the shops so that purchases do not have to be carried far. There is a need for facilities such as public telephones, toilets, baby changing rooms, and refreshments.

Carefully considered shop fronts, tree planting, flower tubs, and litter bins can make the environment more enjoyable to be in. The image of the town can do much to deter vandalism and abuse by encouraging vigilance. Seats and benches allow people to relax during the stressful activity of shopping.

The town will be used by a cross-section of society. Paved and traffic-free areas are welcomed by all. Kerb-stones and narrow passages pose particular difficulties for wheelchair users and those with sight disabilities. Maps, boards, and clear, legible signs are useful to both locals and newcomers to the town.

ASSIGNMENTS

- Find an example of redevelopment in your community. What human factors have been considered by the developers? Have they considered all three types of human factor carefully enough?

What improvements and alterations would you suggest? Use drawing and scale modelling to support your ideas. Ask others to comment on your proposals.

BT public telephone

British Telecom (BT) launched its new range of public telephones in 1986. The new model has a number of distinct advantages over the traditional red box in terms of maintenance and production; but it is worthwhile focusing on the human factors of its design.

The traditional telephone box posed a variety of problems for able and disabled users alike. The heavy door was difficult to open for children and some women. Wheelchair users found it impossible to get near to the phone to dial and insert the coins. The new design, on the other hand, allows easy access to everyone.

The form gives adequate acoustic shielding against disruptive and annoying traffic noise, while at the same time providing temporary shelter. Its open base overcomes the problems of smell and cleaning common with the older design.

British Telecom have maintained a high profile image. The yellow, black, and steel panels are recognizable from a distance – even amongst the confusion of other street furniture and shops.

The telephone itself is fitted with an inductive coupler, to provide clearer speech for people wearing a hearing aid.

The user interface is carefully considered. Clear instructions exploiting both written text and graphic imagery are in full view as you approach the telephone. The sequence of operation is directly stated, and the value of and location for the relevant coins are clearly marked.

The receiver and controls can easily be seen by people of all heights, and telephone directories are readily to hand in secure and robust holders. A small shelf provides a convenient resting place for address boooks, notes, or money that may be required during the phone call.

ASSIGNMENTS

- Try to find an old BT public phone – the sort that is housed in a red box. If you cannot find one, try studying photographs or BT leaflets about the older phones. Draw up a chart to compare the features of the new BT phone with the older version. Which human factors have the designers of each considered? Are there any they have not considered?

- Devise a questionnaire to examine what other people think of the new design. Ask in detail for their opinions of all the ways in which it differs from the old version, and of how easy it is to recognize and use overall. Ask a cross-section of users to complete your questionnaire, and be careful your questions do not bias their answers.

Discuss the findings with other pupils in your class. Is there any feature that is especially liked or disliked? Is there any group of users that especially likes or dislikes the design?

Steam iron

Domestic products have received enormous development in recent years. Not only has the application of high technology revolutionized the potential of consumer products, but the vast numbers in which they are made has resulted in a relatively low cost.

The domestic steam iron has become one of the most popular and versatile electrical items in the home. However, it could be a dangerous one, and major manufacturers have undertaken lengthy research studies into human factors to improve its safety in use.

Like all electrical products, it must conform to European safety standards with regard to materials, components, and assembly. For the user the most important information is likely to be the temperature of the iron, and this is clearly seen from above. A red warning light is used to inform the user that the iron is switched on and is heating up to the pre-set temperature.

The handle has been designed to be comfortable in a wide variety of hand sizes. This and the iron's light weight make it suitable for women and men. The temperature and steam setting can be adjusted without the user putting his or her hand near to the hot base plate, and both provide audible feedback when moved. The iron's angled end allows it to stand safely when not being used, and the shaped moulding provides a location for the coiled flex when not in use. The iron even allows for forgetful users by switching itself off if left face down.

Even well-designed products need to be explained. The iron is supplied with a clear and concise manual that uses graphics to communicate the safe use of the product. Manufacturers are now paying more attention to the human factors of information design when considering instruction manuals. Graphic designers are used for this specialist task.

ASSIGNMENTS

- Find an iron that you can examine in detail. Without taking it apart, examine the human factors of its design. What do you think are its good and bad features?

- How have irons developed this century? Using a library or a museum, investigate the activity of ironing over the past eighty years. Design a chart showing some of the products that have resulted. How do their designs compare with that of a modern steam iron in terms of human factors?

Folding pushchair

The pushchair is one of those products where there are two users to consider – the child and the parent or carer. The infant must be held in place comfortably and safely, with feet well clear of the floor. There must be no sharp edges to metal or plastic components on which to catch small fingers. The materials and fabrics used need to be easily cleanable and provide a warm, comfortably textured finish. Ideally the pushchair should incorporate some adjustment so that it maintains good posture as the child grows.

Negotiating a busy high street or using public transport can pose particularly difficult problems for people with a pushchair. It should be easily manoeuvrable and capable of folding down for transport or storage. On the pushchair in these photographs, the shape and size of the handles conform to a comfortable wrist position for a variety of adults. Height adjustment on the handles reduces backache for the pusher. Straps are easily removed or adjusted. Tubular metal provides a strong frame that is light enough for a woman in the 5%le strength category to lift.

Visually, the pushchair looks strong and secure – an important consideration to parents of young children. The colour scheme is designed to have associations with other modern products, including motor vehicles.

ASSIGNMENTS

- Talk to parents or carers who are responsible for young infants. What is their opinion of the design of pushchairs, prams, etc.? What difficulties have they experienced in this area? What features do they particularly like about the pushchair or pram they use?

- Investigate the range of pushchairs and prams that you can find in local shops. Study them from the point of view of both users – the child and the carer – when the child is being pushed in wet weather, in dry weather, in a busy town, on an uneven surface, etc. Design a poster that is aimed at parents or carers and which highlights a selection of any design faults and good points you have identified. Is there one pushchair or pram that would be best for all users?

Administrative office

Administrative offices have become extremely sophisticated environments in recent years. Advances in information technology have made new aspects of good office design vital. A vast amount of human factors information is available on the best arrangement and use of keyboards, visual display unit (VDU) screens, and traditional working surfaces.

Operators may be male or female, and all equipment must be adjustable to suit each person's requirements. Computer screens should tilt and raise, as should seats, which must ensure adequate lumber support. Castors will allow the chair to move and may reduce fatigue.

Poor lighting is known to create eye strain, headaches, and even serious illness. General and local illumination can help to alleviate this. Similarly, good ventilation and controlled temperature result in a better working environment. The nature of the materials used is an important human factor. Reduction of glare and use of suitable textures can make work more enjoyable.

Proximity to colleagues needs to be considered, and screens can offer privacy in open plan offices. The colour scheme can subconsciously affect people's mood.

ASSIGNMENTS

- Arrange to visit the administrative office of a local company. Ask if you may talk to the people employed in this office about their work requirements, and measure and sketch the room and furniture. How would you improve the human factors of your chosen office? Use models and scale drawings to support your improved design.

- Try to imagine what offices will look like fifty years from now. What human factors will designers need to consider in the office of the future? Illustrate your ideas with scale drawings and models.

Tractor cab

The designer and ergonomist need to work closely together to develop suitable cabin environments for large machinery, such as cranes, lorries, or earth-moving equipment. There are a variety of psychological and physiological human factors that must be taken into account if the driver is to perform complex tasks efficiently. The development team should have access to anthropometric data relevant to the user-group – in this case people (mostly men) between the ages of 18 and 65.

Windows need to offer a good view of the working area, but the size of windows may be affected by the need to reduce vibration and noise. Access must be considered, especially access in an emergency, and therefore doors should not be obstructed. Handles and locks need to be easy to operate. Materials should be chosen to offer a non-slip floor and a non-reflective display, and to make cleaning easy. The development team should also consider the storage of things such as maintenance tools, and even the driver's packed lunch!

The cab itself must be rigid and strong to protect the occupant. The interior layout must allow different operators to sit comfortably with all controls to hand. Stress can be reduced by correct support to arms, legs, and trunk; this may be complicated by overalls, helmets, and other protective clothing. All controls, dials, and warning lights need to be within the operator's field of vision, and also to provide the right type of information for the task. Standard symbols should be used throughout to avoid confusion. Controls need to be easily distinguishable by both sight and touch, and capable of being used even in thick gloves.

ASSIGNMENTS

- Arrange permission to look closely at the cabin of a large machine. A tractor, lorry, or crane would be ideal. Use drawings to show the position of every control the operator might use.

What is the size and shape of the necessary reach envelope (see page 22)? Using waste materials such as cardboard boxes, make a full-size model of the interior of an operator's cabin. Simulate all the controls that would be necessary.

How can you make it suitable for everyone in your class to use?

Computer/human interface

Computer technology has entered all of our lives, whether in using a bank's cash-point machine or playing electronic arcade games. We increasingly have to interact with computers. Ergonomists and designers work together to make the interface between the user and the computer as effective as possible. The software they develop is one product of this, and is likely to involve a detailed analysis of psychological human factors.

For the development team of a product such as a word-processing program there are many problems. The software may be used by people of all ages and a range of abilities. Children may not understand certain commands, while elderly people may have difficulty reading small type. Some people may be used to computers, while others may be just beginning.

The term 'user-friendly' has come into the language to describe software that is easy to work with. This may involve providing help when necessary or being able to go back a stage. Commands and actions should be logical and simple, and symbols should be clear and consistent. The program should relate closely with the keyboard or mouse, so that the user is always in control.

The manuals that are written to support computer software have often received criticism because writers have failed to appreciate the users' basic problems. Jargon and the leaving out of 'obvious' stages are common faults.

ASSIGNMENTS

- Study the design of video games machines, such as those found in amusement arcades. Divide your analysis into two sections – the software (program) and the hardware (machine). What human factors have designers considered in each of these? How well suited are they to their user-group?

- Imagine you have to give a talk to junior pupils on the subject of 'What makes computers user-friendly'. What factors would you identify in your presentation? What examples would you use to illustrate your talk? Plan out your talk, including visual aids such as drawings, photographs, and models.

Hover electric lawnmower

The lesiure time available to many families is increasing, and it seems some of this is aimed at the garden. Producers of lawnmowers and other powered garden products have witnessed a significant rise in demand in recent years.

There have been an alarming number of accidents where people have cut themselves on moving blades – usually a result of not unplugging before turning the machine over. Recent designs have attempted to overcome this through movement indicators mounted in the top of the mower, and through 'on' switches that require two hands to operate.

Muscular fatigue can be reduced if the handles can be adjusted to the correct height. Bright colours are used to denote danger areas, such as the moving parts or the electric cable. Warning labels are positioned where it is difficult not to see them.

The use of 240-volt mains electricity in the garden is a significant potential danger for the user. The risk of electric shock can be minimized by using a circuit breaker, but the designer is obliged to make the product as foolproof and as safe as is reasonably possible. Heavy duty wiring, fuses, and double insulation are part of good design here. Developments in material technology allow manufacturers to fit plastic blades, thus reducing the danger of accidentally cutting through shoes or the trailing flex.

ASSIGNMENTS

- Safety is vital in electrical products. Visit local shops and garden centres and study the electrical garden products. What safety features can you identify in each? What improvements can you suggest? Develop your ideas with drawings and models.

- How safety conscious are most people when working in the garden? Devise a study to examine the risks people take with electrical garden products. Use this to investigate the working practices of a cross-section of gardeners in your community.

Does your investigation suggest that any extra safety features are needed? Design an amended version of one electrical garden product that might increase users' safety.

Going further

Humans are very adaptable beings. We can tolerate a considerable amount of discomfort and inconvenience, particularly if the effort to adapt appears harder than putting up with the discomfort. However, human adaptability should not be an excuse for bad design.

Those responsible for giving form to our products, systems, and environments must exploit the growing research within the human sciences. More work needs to be done to increase designers' awareness of the work of sociologists, ergonomists, and human factors scientists.

Recent government legislation has demanded that manufacturers – and this includes designers – must take greater responsibility for products that do not suit the user or are dangerous. However, it is not only professional designers who need to consider the human factors in their work. Every school design project will interact with people in one way or another, and an understanding of this relationship is vital to the project's success. Human factors are as essential to graphic and textile design as they are to mechanical or electronic design.

There are very few books that discuss this general relationship between design and human factors. There are ones that offer a detailed presentation of human factors research, and these can be of great assistance in particular problems. However, no book can provide you with a checklist of ergonomics considerations for each project. It is this book's intention to provide an overview – the application in project work is up to you.

Design is an activity concerned with modelling, and this may include drawing and mathematics in addition to three-dimensional modelling. The study of human factors also depends upon modelling to apply these factors, and to test and examine their application, in design projects.

User trials are essential to product development. These exploit models ranging from quick and inexpensive lash-ups, such as a simple knife handle in clay, to costly simulations, such as an aircraft cockpit.

There is a great deal of overlap between the physiological, the psychological, and the sociological factors of design. It is likely that many of the design problems you encounter will require you to consider all three areas of human factors that are presented in this book. It is important to identify each influence so that you may work out how it can best be tackled. The examples in this book show how two or more factors can be at work simultaneously, and these may be in conflict or in harmony.

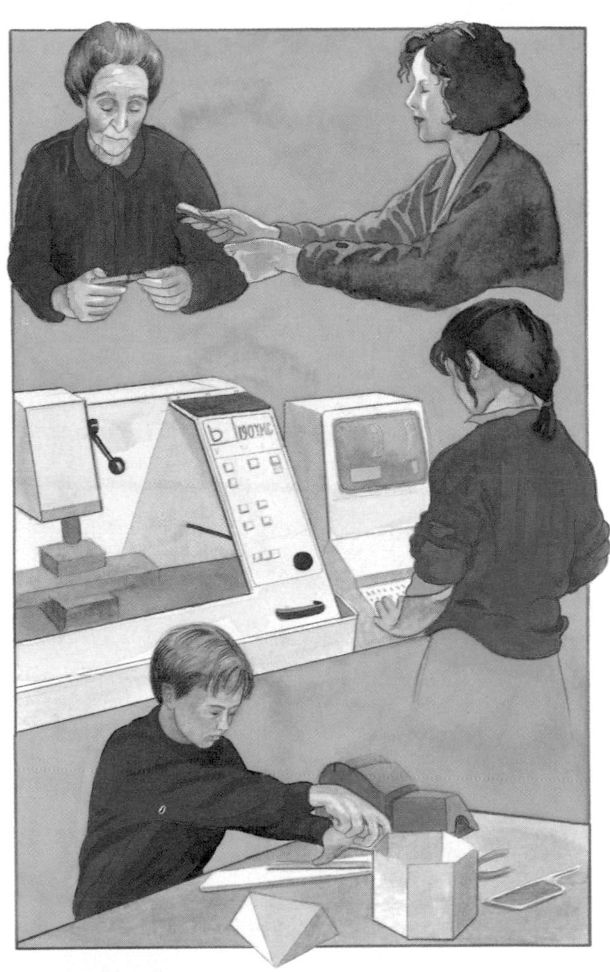

The case studies illustrate this overlap between the three areas of human factors in a range of products. They also reveal the extent to which we have to design for people in all of our items, systems, and environments. Mass production requires us to harness technology in products that suit vast numbers of individuals. Designing with a sensitivity to human factors is likely to become an increasingly important way to do this.

Human measurement guidelines

All measurements are in mm. See page 15 for percentiles (%le).

Girls (14–16 years)					Boys (14–16 years)		
5%le	50%le	95%le		Dimension	5%le	50%le	95%le
1465	1585	1700	A	Standing height	1500	1645	1790
1350	1470	1590	B	Eye level	1380	1530	1675
1180	1285	1395	C	Shoulder height	1215	1345	1480
900	985	1075	D	Elbow height	930	1025	1130
735	810	885	E	Hip height	790	875	965
525	590	660	F	Fingertip height	520	595	665
1440	1575	1710	G	Arm span	1505	1685	1860
750	830	910	H	Elbow span	790	890	990
590	655	720	I	Forward reach	610	690	765
1760	1925	2095	J	Upward reach	1830	2010	2185
765	830	895	K	Sitting height	765	850	930
655	720	780	L	Sitting eye level	655	735	810
170	220	270	M	Sitting elbow height	175	225	270
385	420	455	N	Elbow to fingertips	400	445	495
115	140	165	O	Thigh clearance	115	140	170
445	495	535	P	Knee to floor	470	525	575
330	380	425	Q	Standard seat height	355	405	460
415	465	510	R	Seat length	410	465	520
340	385	425	S	Shoulder breadth	355	405	460
280	330	380	T	Hip breadth	265	310	360
155	175	180	V	Hand length	160	180	200
70	75	80	W	Hand breadth	75	85	95

Women (19–65 years)					Men (19–65 years)		
5%le	50%le	95%le		Dimension	5%le	50%le	95%le
1505	1610	1710	A	Standing height	1625	1740	1855
1390	1490	1595	B	Eye level	1510	1625	1745
1210	1310	1410	C	Shoulder height	1310	1415	1525
905	980	1060	D	Elbow height	995	1080	1165
745	815	885	E	Hip height	830	910	995
540	595	650	F	Fingertip height	580	640	705
1460	1595	1730	G	Arm span	1645	1785	1925
815	890	960	H	Elbow span	880	960	1040
665	725	785	I	Forward reach	715	780	850
1880	2030	2180	J	Upward reach	2040	2195	2350
790	845	900	K	Sitting height	850	910	970
685	740	790	L	Sitting eye level	740	800	860
185	225	265	M	Sitting elbow height	190	240	285
405	440	475	N	Elbow to fingertips	430	470	510
105	140	170	O	Thigh clearance	125	150	175
455	495	535	P	Knee to floor	495	540	590
340	380	420	Q	Standard seat height	365	415	460
430	480	535	R	Seat length	440	495	550
370	415	460	S	Shoulder breadth	415	460	500
320	375	430	T	Hip breadth	315	360	400
155	170	185	V	Hand length	175	190	205
70	75	85	W	Hand breadth	80	90	95

Outlines of ergonomes

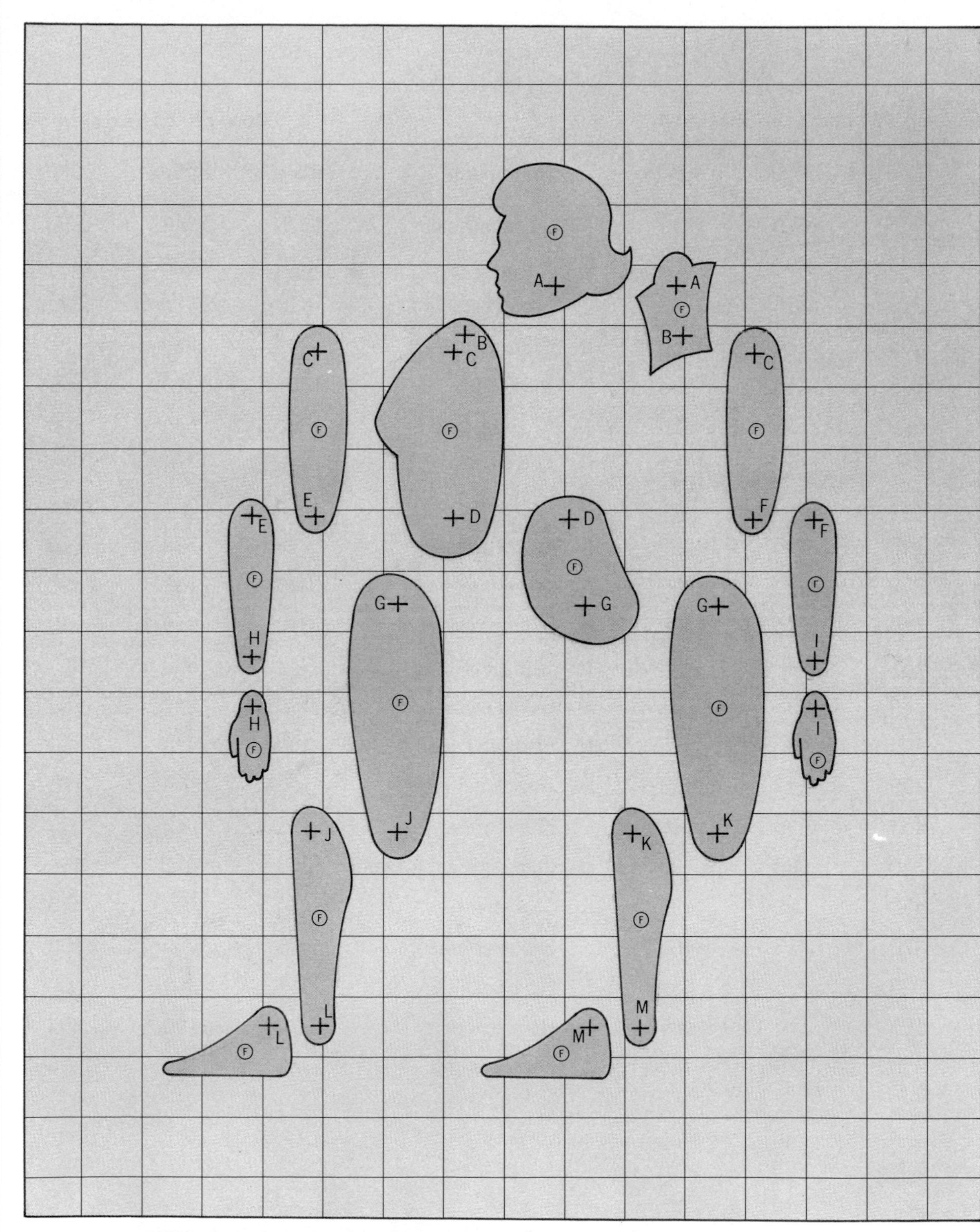

Ergonome of 5%le female in the 19–65 age group (scale 1:10)

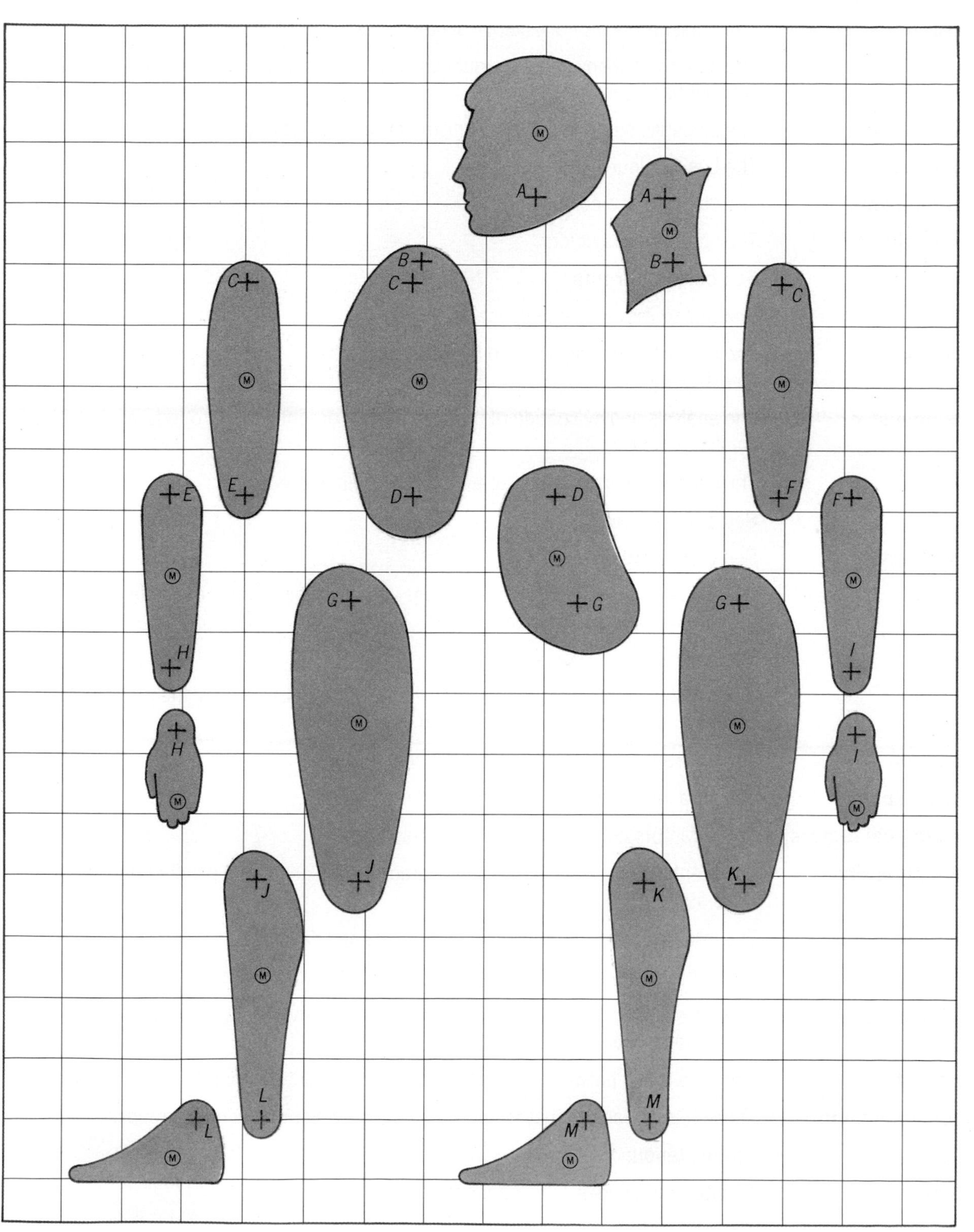

Ergonome of 95%le male in the 19–65 age group (scale 1:10)

Glossary

Anthropometrics The measurement of physiological human factors.

Average The sum total of any given quantity divided by the number of components from which it has been derived.

Biomechanics The scientific study of the mechanism of the human body.

Colour hue The basic colour – red, green, etc.

Colour chroma The strength of a colour.

Colour value The lightness of a colour.

Chroma See **colour chroma**.

Dynamic Relating to movement or space.

Ergonome The movable scale figure used by designers to assist with human factors investigation.

Ergonomics The analysis and evaluation of products, environments, and procedures that involve people.

Feedback The sensory information received in reply to an action.

Hue See **colour hue**.

Human factors See **ergonomics**.

Interface The place of contact or relationship between two things – for example, between people and products.

Mean See **average**.

Percentile A point on a graph, divided regularly into 100 groups, revealing the probability of human characteristics for a defined population.

Perception The awareness of information via the senses.

Personal space The area immediately surrounding our bodies.

Physiological factors Those factors concerned with the human body.

Product identity The identifiable and distinguishing characteristics given to a product during development.

Product semantics The interpretation of meaning in the form of any design.

Psychological factors Those human factors that require or involve interpretation by the brain.

Reach envelope The physical area of influence of a given person – everything he or she can comfortably reach.

Reaction time The time taken between sensing information and acting upon it.

Sociological factors Those human factors that result from people living or working in groups.

Static Still or stationary.

System An integrated series of component parts.

Value See **colour value**.

QUEEN'S GATE SCHOOL
133 QUEEN'S GATE
LONDON SW7 5LE
TELEPHONE: 01-589 3587